BEYOND DISCIPLESHIP
— to —
RELATIONSHIP

Developing Intimacy with the Lord

BARBARA A. F. BREHON

WestBow
PRESS
A DIVISION OF THOMAS NELSON
& ZONDERVAN

Copyright © 2014 Barbara A. F. Brehon.

All rights reserved. No part of this book may be used or reproduced by any means, graphic, electronic, or mechanical, including photocopying, recording, taping or by any information storage retrieval system without the written permission of the publisher except in the case of brief quotations embodied in critical articles and reviews.

WestBow Press books may be ordered through booksellers or by contacting:

WestBow Press
A Division of Thomas Nelson & Zondervan
1663 Liberty Drive
Bloomington, IN 47403
www.westbowpress.com
1 (866) 928-1240

Because of the dynamic nature of the Internet, any web addresses or links contained in this book may have changed since publication and may no longer be valid. The views expressed in this work are solely those of the author and do not necessarily reflect the views of the publisher, and the publisher hereby disclaims any responsibility for them.

ISBN: 978-1-4908-2967-8 (sc)
ISBN: 978-1-4908-2968-5 (hc)
ISBN: 978-1-4908-2966-1 (e)

Library of Congress Control Number: 2014904633

Printed in the United States of America.

WestBow Press rev. date: 03/20/2014

Contents

Preface xi
Acknowledgments xiii
Introduction xv
    Cut Off but Grafted In xvi

Individual Discipleship
"I want to grow."

Part 1

Broken Pieces 3
    Shifts in Seasons 3
    Clay Can Be Reshaped 5
    Repurposed Broken Pieces 6
    Purpose and Believing 7
    Distractions and Purpose 8
    Leftovers Have Value 9
Block Me from Me 12
    Decide to Abide 12
    Temple Maintenance: Be a Body Builder 17
Connect with Christ 21
    To Know Christ 22
    To Know the Power of His Resurrection 23
    To Know the Fellowship of His Sufferings 25
    To Be Conformed to His Death 25

Part 2

Build Relationships 28
    Tap into the Power Source 28
    The Best Ministry Approach 30
    Inside Relationships 31

Get a Grip 35
    Christian Integrity 36
    Christian Identity 36
    Christian Intelligence 37
Biblical Paradigms 39
    According to Matthew 39
    According to John 41
    The Great Commission According to Matthew, Mark, Luke, and John 42
    A Fruit-Bearing Vision 44
    Biblical Triads 46

Spiritual Mentoring and Leadership

"I want to help others grow."

Part 3

Ministering to Growing Disciples 53
    Attrition 55
Discipling Dilemma 57
    Stagnant 58
    Getting Started Personally 62
    Getting Started Corporately 62
Merging Processes 66
    Design 66
    Observations from Experiential Encounters 71
    Summary of the Encounters 74
    Collegial Support 76

Part 4

Reckoning 81
    Strengths 83
    Weaknesses 84
    Recommendations 85
    Suggestions 85
Conclusion 87

There Is a Balm in Gilead 88

    Background of the Lyrics 88
    John 17: Jesus' Prayer 89
Appendix 1 – The Seven Session Components 91

Appendix 2 – "Maturing as a Christian" Course Review 95
Appendix 3 – "Maturing as a Christian" Evaluation Form 96
Appendix 4 – Experiential Encounters Journal 98
Notes 117

Bibliography 119
More from the Author 121
About the Author 123

Photographs by the Author

Cover	–	"Mountaintop Experience" Greece, 2004
Page 1	–	"Though Broken" Essex County, Virginia, 2009
Page 6	–	"Shine Through Storms" Hanover, Virginia, at sunrise, August 2011
Page 14	–	"Solitude by the Sea" Fort De Soto, Florida, June 2013
Page 20	–	"Another Mountaintop Experience" over the Swiss Alps, November 2004
Page 24	–	"Resurrection" Church of the Ascension, Holy Land, 2003
Page 37	–	"Who Made the Sun?" Greece, November 2004
Page 51	–	"Return from the mountain top to be poured out for the Lord" Greece, November 2004
Page 79	–	"Sunset" Virginia Beach, Virginia

Preface

I have written *Beyond Discipleship to Relationship* to inspire individual intimacy with the Lord. Many Christians have decided to seriously follow Jesus while meeting in small, intimate groups of people with whom they are familiar. Anyone who wants to grow and wants to help others to grow in the Lord will find a practical approach that can be replicated. This book is not just for ministry and lay leaders but for anyone interested in a more intimate relationship with Christ. I encourage Christians to revitalize themselves by imitating the gospel story so that others will see Christ in their lives. This developmental approach will nudge them toward spiritual growth and establish nurturing partnerships within congregations. Church members will be motivated to become more involved in ministries, and the church will grow from the inside out.

Acknowledgments

I thank my Lord, Jesus Christ, for allowing me to draw closer to him. I am grateful for having had parents, the late Richard and Jerlean Fields, who instilled the importance of governing my life according to a standard of excellence.

I extend heartfelt gratitude to Evelyn Fields, Carolyn Pope, Raymond Whitaker, and Ramona Garner, who read portions of *Beyond Discipleship to Relationship* and offered valuable reflections. I am appreciative of Gregory Brehon, who allowed me to use his photograph of his winning entry in a pumpkin-carving contest. I also thank Annette Riley, Ette' Photography, for the photograph used with my biography.

Introduction

I was in church all my life, but I was lonely. I had to decide to do something about my situation because no one was going to do it for me. Change came gradually; it certainly didn't happen overnight. Looking back, I realize that my circumstances didn't improve until I got into the Word, studying for myself what it said instead of relying on preachers and teachers to interpret it for me. I was lonely until I started associating with people who were like what I wanted to become. I began taking responsibility for my growth and let others help me. I had to shed attitudes, thoughts, and behaviors as I became aware that they were hindering me. I had to practice being what I hoped to be.

Christians must accept responsibility for their growth. Peter ends his second letter by telling us to grow in grace and knowledge of our Lord and Savior Jesus Christ (2 Peter 3:18). I know that this grace is God's special gift. He allows us to walk in his favor.

When the soul is at peace, we position ourselves for intimacy with the Lord. Our focus shifts from the concerns that made us seek comfort to the need for divine direction each minute of the day. We can move beyond discipleship to a deeper relationship with the Lord when we sit with him regularly to learn his ways, then practice them. Yes, Jesus is the soothing balm that heals our wounds whether they be physical, emotional, or spiritual. He comforts us and brings peace to the soul. The Lord tells us to come to him when we are weary and burdened because he will give us rest. God wants us to learn from him and find rest for our souls. (Matthew 11:28–29).

Throughout this book, I will offer opportunities for self-reflection in sections headed "Personal Points to Ponder."

Cut Off but Grafted In

To become mature Christians, we must be implanted into the Tree of Life. We must be grafted in Jesus. Our faith does this. The idea of grafting came to me from reading Romans 11, which says that the Gentiles came to know salvation despite their transgressions. I thought about being broken and repurposed, and I revisited this narrative. Paul describes the process of salvation, helping us to envision our purpose and where we fit in.

Paul assumed that those living in the region were familiar with grafting olive trees, which I saw all over the Holy Land when I visited. Grafting these trees is a common practice. The wild olive trees are cut back, slits are made on the freshly sawed branch ends, and two or three grafts from a cultivated olive tree are inserted so that the bark from the cut portion and the bark from the branch coincide. The exposed ends are smeared with mud made from clay, then bound with cloth or straw. The fruit obtained this way is good. Wild olives cannot be made cultivated olives by engrafting, as Paul implies, but a wild olive branch can be grafted and thrive. Likewise, Gentiles would flourish spiritually when grafted into the fullness of God's mercy, first revealed to the world through Israel. Grafting and grace—what an empowering thought! Though broken, we all have a chance to be repaired.

The Jews were like cultured seeds that took root and grew up with a heritage of faithful fathers, patriarchs of our faith. However, the Gentiles were like an attached rootstock. They were a cutting with roots. They were foreign to the faith. Unbelief cuts us off from God, who is our rootstock. Faith grafts us in to salvation through Christ. Whether we grew up in the faith or were grafted in through experience, what matters is that circumstances, our seasons in life, bring us to our purpose for being. We are grafted by grace. At times we must admit our ignorance of what God is doing. We must submit to his will so he can repurpose us, remold us, take our broken pieces, and use them for his glory. Being repurposed is not a bad thing at all. God grants his grace for us to be grafted into his kingdom.

But once grafting takes place, all is not automatically well. There is more work to be done. The grafted branch must be wrapped up, but an opening must be provided for moisture to get in a couple of times a week. The graft cannot produce water on its own. In the same way, Christians must take part in Bible study to be nurtured for effective use in the fields where they are planted.

Looking at this analogy, keep in mind that several branches are grafted with the understanding that not all of them will take root and thrive. You nurture the branch regularly, but you do not pester it by continually pulling at the cloth to see what is going on inside. Pests, weather, and accidents take a toll on new trees, new members, new converts, babes in Christ who may have occupied the same pew in the same church for years. After the grafting, wait a year or so and plant the graft in the orchard with other trees of like kind. In the church setting, help the babe attach to a ministry based on God's gifts of grace. The graft may not bear fruit for several years, but it has fertile ground in which to grow and to produce every year in its season.

You can take a wild branch and graft it to a cultivated rootstock so that the wild one produces a different quality of fruit. Repurpose it for a new season. That wild branch might be you. Allow yourself to be grafted. Let your untamed nature become wrapped up in someone with roots deeply embedded in the Lord. This will help you stay grounded. As a graft, you are not seasoned or nurtured from the root, but you can become attached to someone with deep roots. As you continue growing in faith, you eventually produce desirable fruit to help build God's kingdom. Knowledge of God has deep riches of wisdom. (Romans 11:33).

You may find yourself outside of your biological family but grafted into the fellowship of believers in Christ. This is disciple making. Somebody shared with you and listened to you. In turn, you allowed yourself to be the branch grafted into a new lifestyle.

When you disciple others and mentor them, you do not know what will be produced. You plant the seeds, another waters them, and God gives the increase (1 Corinthians 3:6–7). You do not know the outcome, but you must be obedient to spread the Word. When you focus on a mission from the Lord, you see your brokenness differently. It becomes a seed to be nurtured. Brokenness is an opportunity for a more seasoned saint to escort you through your current situation toward your destiny. That brokenness later gives you a tool to connect with someone else and usher that person to a seat of salvation and peace in knowing Jesus. God's promises are irrevocable, and time will prove it. Build slowly and grow through this season to the next. Cut yourself off from sin and attach yourself to him.

Personal Points to Ponder
Grafting and grace—What are they to you?
Grafting—To what person or organization are you or will you become spiritually attached?
Grace—What are the spiritual gifts you offer in service to the Lord?

Being interconnected provides strength and stability, allowing roots to become more deeply embedded in the soil of faith. This book is intended for longtime church members who seek persons active in their faith to help them develop a more intimate relationship with Christ. People cannot do this on their own. Those attempting to deepen their relationship with Christ must be held accountable for producing evidence of growth into Christian maturity. Accountability carries reciprocal responsibility; each side in the relationship has a duty. At the same time, both are nurtured with spiritual intimacy. It is important that the participant choose the mentor. This will allow emotional safety for sharing.

The chief goal is to provide opportunities for growth. Church members interested in Christian progress can mature at many levels. With this in mind, participants should become more involved in church ministries. In doing so, they will find a place where they can confide in each other regarding issues of personal development. While growing themselves, these disciples will be moved to assist others in deepening their relationships with God.

Individual Discipleship

"I want to grow."

Discipleship is a choice that individuals make to live in a Christ-like manner, and churches must provide support for those persons. The call to discipleship is personal whereas disciple-making involves reaching others so they may grow in relationship with Christ. Discipleship is a first step in the process of maturing as a Christian and developing a personal relationship with God through Jesus Christ. Every process involves steps and takes time; it is sequential and must be intentional. You must be conscious of what you are doing; actions won't take place by themselves.

A disciple is a learner in the process of becoming spiritually mature. A Christian disciple is a follower of Jesus Christ and student of the Word of God. When disciples not only nurture their relationships with Christ but also help others be more Christ-like, they become disciple-makers.

Discipleship is a lifelong commitment to a lifestyle rather than to a program or a ministry.[1] Rather than simply leading them in completing a short-term regimen of tasks and responsibilities covered in a class, true discipleship helps people devoted to a lifelong journey imitate Jesus Christ. A disciple-maker engages "the whole process … of reaching the lost with the gospel, discipling people in their intimacy and walk with Christ."[2] Discipleship is faith expressed in practice.[3]

PART 1

**Broken Pieces
Block Me from Me
Connect with Christ**

"Though Broken"
Essex County, Virginia, 2009

Broken Pieces

Anyone born has been broken at one time or another. However, that does not mean that you must continue to live as a broken vessel. The Lord can graft you back into fellowship and sweet communion with the Holy Spirit. You may feel like somebody's leftovers. You may have felt that what you had to offer had no value or was not valued. But leftovers have value. You may think that your turn will never come. But seasons change, so be encouraged.

If you feel like you have been used and abused, remember that clay can be reshaped. If you believe that you have no purpose, recognize that you do. You can uncover that purpose. Broken pieces can be repurposed. You may be a broken branch, but you can be grafted into the tree of everlasting life. However, you do not have to do this on your own; a branch does not graft itself. We will explore examples of brokenness, knowing that everybody can be restored to wholeness. It is the Lord's will that none perish. The Lord is patient and wants everyone to repent. (2 Peter 3:9).

Shifts in Seasons

When times are more difficult, we must trust God more. Learning to depend on God's promises isn't always easy. A lady once told me that she had been praying often for more patience. She mentioned the many times when she needed more of this virtue. The Spirit prompted me to tell her that God was answering her continual prayer by giving her chances to use that gift.

How can you get better at something without opportunities to practice it? Never give up on your circumstances. Galatians 6:9 says that we must not become weary; do not give up. Harvest time ends one season only to begin another. Turn to the source of power for strength. Lamentations 3:22–23 helps us to understand that we are not used up. God has never-ending compassion that never fails. We must wake up every morning saying that God is great and faithful.

God also gives us persons I like to call "intimate others" to help us when we are at our weakest and lowest moments. They will not necessarily give us money or remove our woes, but we will not have to go hungry or beg for anything. As Psalm 37:25 reminds us that the righteous will not be forsaken and will not have to beg for bread.

You are not under a curse, just in a difficult season of life. Do not feel that you must be there alone. Share your concerns with your inner circle, those intimate others who form your triad (three people like Jesus had in Peter, James, and John). There you will find strength for the journey. (Matthew 18:20).

Faced with shifting seasons, consider God's plan. There are times when you must have your own money, food, and clothing, and there are times when you must allow others to provide these things. God not only provides for you, but he sets up situations so Christ's followers can be a blessing to others. Pride or a desire for privacy can make receiving difficult, but God will lead you every step of the way as you enter a more intimate relationship with him.

I once went three-and-a-half years without a job. I was a theological student and did ministry full time. Times got rough, but God never allowed me to miss a meal and always kept a roof over my head. I had decent clothes to wear for every occasion, and I remained healthy with no need to pay for doctors or prescriptions. I had to set priorities and decide what would take me closer to my goals. As you grow in the Lord, life's circumstances will strengthen your testimony. Listen to others and share your testimony, knowing that God works in different ways in each of us.

As you listen and share, be mindful that you always have a choice. No one can make you think anything you do not want to think, any more than you can make another person think, do, or be what you want. You cannot change anyone but yourself. What did Jesus say about your situation? Find out from his Word and from others who know the Word. You can control what you think by choosing what you believe. But what are you feeding your mind? Garbage in, garbage out; negativity in, negativity out. If you keep doing the same thing the same way, you will keep getting the same result.

Being seasoned for Christ means honoring him even through strenuous financial seasons. Jesus instructed his disciples not to take anything with them when they went out to do kingdom work. (Luke 9:3 and Mark 6:8–11). However, before his crucifixion, Jesus told them to take their purse, bag, and sword. (Luke 22:35–38). The times had changed.

No contradiction exists here if you comprehend the nature of seasons. There are seasons of want and seasons of plenty. There is a time for everything. (Ecclesiastes 3:1). Knowing that things do not stay the same, you must prepare for the season that lies ahead. Your lack of preparation will not stop it from coming. But you always have a choice.

While Jesus was with the disciples in the flesh, he knew that they would be persecuted once he had left and that even those who might want to help would not for fear of their lives. There will always come a time when your worldly resources will be sparse, but never compare your circumstances to those of others. As a disciple of Christ, you must be vigilant, preparing for times of want and times of plenty. Rethink your situation. What might God be doing for you through it all? Paul told one church that he knew what it was like to be in need and to have plenty. But he discovered contentment. (Philippians 4:12).

You need not continue to live as a broken vessel. You will survive to share your story and to enjoy more intimate moments with the Lord.

Clay Can Be Reshaped

You can be remolded to do even greater works than Christ. (John 14:12). One of the greatest challenges for me was to change my thinking. I had to redefine myself, to live based on what I believed, and to make sure I could back up every action with the Bible. Let God be God in your life. He is the potter. (Isaiah 64:8). Pray for his will and let it be done. When you are flawed, he can and will fix it according to what he thinks is best. (Jeremiah 18:4 and Romans 9:20–21). Circumstances do change.

Barbara A. F. Brehon

Repurposed Broken Pieces

The Lord can use the broken, as can men. In Acts 27:39–44, those who can swim do just that, but those who cannot swim make it safely to shore on the broken pieces of a ship destroyed by a storm.

"Shine through Storms"
Hanover, Virginia, at sunrise, August 2011

The men would have lost their lives if they had not clung to the boards that once made up the ship. Each plank was repurposed and redefined. You must redefine yourself to align with God's purpose for creating you. Recognize who you are in the Lord because God is worthy to receive glory and honor and power, for he created all things by his will (Revelation 4:11). You have purpose. You are useful.

You must know your purpose as the Lord knew his. If you are indeed his follower, you cannot remain confused about what you were created to do. If you do not know, ask in Jesus' name and the Holy Spirit will reveal it to you. Then use your gift or mixture of gifts to glorify God. Jesus was certain about his purpose. (Mark 1:38, 10:44–45; Luke 19:10; 24:46–47 and John 12:27). John the Baptist and the twelve disciples knew and followed through with their purpose. (John 1:31). Jesus told the disciples exactly how to serve him and where to go. (Matthew 10:5–6).

Personal Points to Ponder

What does God want you to do? How does God want you to do it? Reflect on your dreams, your hopes, and your desires. What are they?
Dreams:
Hopes:
Desires:
What is God saying about those thoughts and feelings right now? Write them now for later meditation.

Purpose and Believing

John 1:7, 3:16–17, 6:38–39

While it is important to know what you are supposed to do, it is equally imperative that you understand what you are not supposed to do. Jesus makes this clear in Mark 2:17 when he said he did not come to call the righteous, but sinners. I am certain that I am not the only one who has been asked to do something I did not choose to do. For various reasons, you may not want to commit to a task. Others do not always know your purpose.

I once joined a civic organization. Before I attended the first meeting, I was told that a certain position was available. I knew within my spirit this was not my purpose for being a part of the group. Several months later on the day of elections and installation of officers, I was given another opportunity to step up to the plate. Knowing my reasons for being in the group and being assured of my purpose, I did not submit. I did not affiliate for that purpose but for other reasons.

Barbara A. F. Brehon

Distractions and Purpose

When you decide to become more intimate with Jesus, do not be dismayed when the people closest to you do not get what you are doing. Jesus had been accepted by people all over Galilee. However, he stayed away from Judea on purpose (John 7:1–14). His own brothers did not understand him. They tried to get him to attend a town festival in Judea so people could see him do miracles. Have you ever had family members want to put you on display? This showed Jesus that his brothers did not believe in him. I encourage you to know your purpose and be able to stand on it. Lovingly tell others that they can do what they want, but you do not choose to join them because it is not the right time for you. Jesus eventually went in secret and showed himself when he was ready, but some people still would not believe.

If relatives cut you off and no longer include you in family functions, remember that Jesus will never do that. He prayed for you before you were born (John 17:20). Thank you, Lord. You must forgive and pray for others. Many times they will come around with the time-honored evidence of your sincerity. People closest to you will sometimes find it difficult to grasp how you redefined yourself to align with your faith. Some things take more time than others. Look at how much time it took you to decide that you needed to change from the inside out.

You don't need validation by others. Instead you must validate the testimony of your life in Christ so that others can believe through your example (John 5:30–32). Christ has given you the authority to be confident in who you are (John 8:14). Jesus was about to speak the truth to the Pharisees at the temple. He did not need to go to the festival and make a haughty public display, doing miracles as if he were entertaining people at a magic show.

When you walk worthily in the sight of the Lord, some will question you and your intentions. This shouldn't lead you to question yourself. Instead you should feel confident that they are recognizing the Lord's authority in you. Should you respond to the skeptics? What did Jesus say and do? Luke 20:1–8, Matthew 21:23–27, and Mark 11:27–33 offer answers.

The chief priests and the teachers of the law, together with the elders, approached Jesus while he was preaching and demanded to know who gave him the authority to do this. Jesus' reply caused them to question themselves; they assumed he was up to trickery, because that was their agenda. Ultimately, they decided that the best strategy was to tell Jesus they did not know the answer to the question he asked them. Therefore, Jesus did not tell them whose authority he acted upon.

Sometimes you can more easily avoid other people's traps by limiting your response. Let their issues remain with them. You are busy building the kingdom, and you have too much work to do to allow distractions from your mission. Some will not believe in what you are trying to accomplish for the Lord. Stand on Mark 16:16. You know the truth, so pray for these people and move on with your work. Believe that you have received whatever you ask in prayer. (Mark 11:24–25).

To grasp the reality of belief, read the book of John, paying special attention to chapter 6. Christians must understand that not everyone who professes the Lord is a believer. That's true even of those in church. In John 6:64 Jesus said that there are some who do not believe.

Do not allow distractions to deter you from your praise, worship, and mission for the Lord. I once read Scripture over the phone to someone, then prayed with her that she would know when to let go of behavior not substantiated in the Bible. She had asked if I knew where her concern was addressed in the Word. I did not. Folks can try to make you believe that what they are doing is right. Ask them to show you where in the Bible they saw the justification for their actions. Know on what you stand. You do not have to justify yourself or argue any point with others. There will always be those who do not believe as you do and do not live by the same precepts. You must not expect them to make decisions the way you do or to understand what you think is best.

Leftovers Have Value

Has somebody tried to manipulate, control, or bully you? Have you ever felt like you were only someone's afterthought? Perhaps others have said certain things to make you think less of yourself and make themselves feel bigger and better. Maybe others have identified a personal characteristic as your "button" and pushed it as often as they could to keep you where they wanted you. Possibly they included you only after no one else would accept what they proposed. Maybe they sought to entice you to choose them or their way. Perhaps you have encountered people who seemed to get a kick out of making you feel like a leftover. Know that Romans 8:28 is true. All things do work together for good. Know that God has given you hindsight paired with spiritual insight to clearly discern trickery. When you know your purpose, Jesus affirms you on every step of your journey.

Your life may seem fragmented at times. Maybe people have treated you poorly. But think about what the disciples did with the leftovers after feeding the multitude. What happened to the broken pieces that remained? Matthew 14:13–21 and Mark 6:41–44 tell the story about Jesus feeding the five thousand from five loaves and two fish. Matthew 15:32–37 and Mark 8:4–8 offer an account of feeding four thousand with seven loaves and a few small fish. Mark says that the people ate and were satisfied. John 6:12 reveals what happened to the leftovers. They did not throw any of it away. Jesus wanted to purpose the food for later use. Though you have been broken, battered, or scarred, the future awaits you. God can use whoever you have been to help you be better than you were. Use discernment and wisdom in the Lord to detect unnecessary and unwanted leavening in your bread. What makes your yeast rise? Recognize this and deal with it as the Lord directs. When you know the Word of God, you can discern false teachings and prophecies. (Refer to Matthew 16:12 and Mark 8:15, 21 about Herod, the Pharisees, and the Sadducees.)

Did the disciples pick up the broken pieces and throw them away? Of course not. God does not consider anything in his creation a waste. I am not a waste. You are not a waste. Even in our brokenness, we can be gathered and reshaped, reformed, molded again, or grafted into what God intended in the first place. Leftovers have value. Since Jesus is the bread of life, let him feed your spirit. (John 6:35). Since Jesus is the living water, allow him to quench your thirst. (John 4). Do not throw yourself away, and be careful not to toss others aside. We are all works in progress. Growing intimacy with the Lord is a process.

Personal Points to Ponder

What makes your yeast rise? Be honest about identifying the triggers that set you off or make you feel poorly about yourself.

How can you use your worst situation in service to the Lord?

Block Me from Me

Lord, I praise you for being all-powerful. Block me, Lord, I pray, because you promised that you would shield me from harm. Block me, Lord, because you promised that you would fight my battles for me. I confess, Lord, that one of my most harmful foes is myself. Block me, protect me, from me. Thank you, Lord, for being so available to me. I want to get out of your way and be available to you. In Jesus' precious name. Amen.

Jesus prayed for his disciples for protection from evil. (John 17:15). What a pity it is when we allow the enemy to take hold of us. What a shame it is when we forget that the devil will still do that to us even when we consider ourselves holy. My favorite prayer in the Bible is the one found in John prior to Jesus' arrest and crucifixion. His prayer reminds me that the enemy is always on the job and can get to me because I am still in this world. So I pray that the Lord continue to guard me from myself, especially when the devil has a hold of me and I cannot detect it. Protect me, Lord, from me.

Decide to Abide

Abide so deeply in the Lord that you will ask him to be sovereign and block you from yourself. It is wonderful to realize that you do not have to decide anything and that you can simply follow the Lord. Release yourself from self-imposed pressure to make decisions that are not yours to make. Give yourself permission to abide in him and let him guide you in everything. Jesus said to abide in him. To abide means to be in a place, to live there. Be in Christ (John 15:7). Decide to abide. Christians who abide in Christ respect God's sovereignty. God can do what he wants to do because he is sovereign. Therefore, accept his authority over everything. Intimacy with the Father through the Son as led by the Spirit of the living God will allow you to do this.

There are times when you are repentant and say, "I'm sorry, Lord." You do not want to repeat errors. You have no desire to sin. But one thing or one person can get to you like nothing else can. To keep the enemy at bay, I decided to pray more frequently, "Lord, please block me from me. Your ways are not my ways, and your thoughts are not my thoughts. I am not capable of knowing what you know. Please, Lord, block me from me. I am not strong enough to make it through this journey. You must keep me from self-destruction. I choose to abide in you, Jesus." Repentance strengthens a person's relationship with God and is a daily necessity.

I recently endured a strenuous week. Near the end of it, I realized I was showing physical signs of stress. Having survived one heart attack induced by chronic stress, I was not about to wait for another to happen. I prayed, "Lord, show me what I need to do to feel your presence and to know your will. What do you want me to do?" I sequestered myself in my own home and listened to God. He showed me myself and how I had brought on the stress. I had put unnecessary timetables in place and pressured myself. Neither the Lord nor any other human being had done this. I had! Before the end of one day at home, each physical symptom was gone. Lord, continue to block me from me.

After self-imposed isolation, I bounced back. I got a grip on reality. No one asked me to put all that stuff on my plate after I had emptied it only a few months before. I refilled the plate. I became overwhelmed. I had to back up and regroup. Thank you, Lord, for blocking me from me. Sequestering myself restored my balance. I am thankful that I could regroup in less than a week. Earlier in my life the process took years. My relationship with the Lord was suffering, and I missed my time with him. Sometimes I need to steal away to be with Jesus. After I had sat with the Word and done spiritual as well as regular laundry, God let me rest—no face in the computer or a book, no Bible study or sermon preparation, no great thoughts, just sitting. I rode horses with Ben Cartwright and his boys. I watched reruns of *Bonanza*, *The Virginian*, and *High Chaparral*, and the movie *A Fistful of Dollars* in my easy chair.

What relaxes you? Watching westerns transports me to another time. Picturing places that remind me of God's awesome nature recenters and relaxes me.

"Solitude by the Sea"
Fort De Soto, Florida, June 2013

    Playing Words with Friends, Words of Wonder, and Quiddler also relaxes me. There are other times when flower gardening or Yoqua (yoga in the water) at the fitness center will do it. But this time God said, "Just sit." Stop, look at yourself, and listen to whatever God is saying. I needed to rest my mind, eyes, and body. I had to limit almost all activity and conversations. I also had to adjust my eating to hear God. Fasting can take many forms. God will tell you what to avoid and for how long to become re-centered in him. Decide to abide in Jesus.

    I used to think I was handling life pretty well until a doctor told me I had had a heart attack. Who has a heart attack without knowing it until undergoing a routine physical? I did. My vital signs were good; the doctor attributed it to stress. I asked, "Lord, show me when it happened and why it happened so that I can prevent it from happening again."

    Three years after that traumatic event, my annual cardiology visit ended with the same doctor telling me that I did not need him anymore. I was reminded of the time when Jesus said that the sick need a doctor. (Matthew 9:12). I will forever praise the Lord for this. The cardiologist did not say I was stressed. He politely said, "You're very focused." What joy filled me that day! I could have skipped like a little girl out of that office. The doctor who had told me to bring someone with me on every visit now said not to return unless I needed him. "Lord, block me from myself when I am too focused on the wrong thing." We must be attentive to how much focus we put on our own agendas, those items others impose on us, or certain people in our lives. Sometimes we put people before God. We hang on to grudges against those we think wronged us, and we will not address these feelings, let alone forgive.

I pray that the Lord will remove from me anything not aligned with his perfect will. This includes anything I may want or think. I asked God, "How have you blocked me from me?" These are examples he brought to mind.

- I got a flat tire on the way to visit someone at a church. I cannot say that the flat was or was not in God's will. I will not say that a visit is a bad thing. But, I can say that God did not like my motive. After AAA got me on my way, I heeded the warning and did not make that visit.
- Driving to a friend's house, I got the distinct feeling that something could happen to me and no one would know where I was or how to find me. God gives us warning signals. I got the internal discomfort that comes when God is speaking to me. When I arrived, I did not feel a sense of relief. I knew I did not need to return.
- My car had been in my garage since I had last parked it. I got two flat tires at the same time on the driver's side before turning the corner leading out of my neighborhood. That prevented me from doing a leadership workshop at a church. Later the pastor and I understood that he needed to lead that session. Comments and questions by a church leader unexpectedly revealed a hostile attitude toward the pastor. The moderator of a meeting is not the only one who shows up with an agenda, though it might be hidden.
- It is interesting to note the number of spiritual moments I have had while driving. God showed me that my heart attack occurred

while I was driving home. I used a routine route and happened to be at an intersection not far from the hospital. I prayed for the Lord to heal me of whatever was happening so that I would not harm others on the road. The sensation in my arms and my hands and the squeezing in my chest stopped. I thanked the Lord, drove through the traffic light, and went home, not knowing the gravity of what had just happened.

- I once clearly saw a snake coming toward me in a dream. When I showed no fear, the snake disappeared. A snake is the one thing that horrifies me. Yet, I was not afraid. I awoke and heard a voice clearly say, "Get out of this den of iniquity." God allowed me to experience what he wanted, then told me to leave. Thank you, Lord, for protection. Three months or so later, I had another dream associated with the same place. I awoke asking why I dreamed about it. I decided that the dream was a reminder to stay away from this place. I know the thought came from God. I have since deleted information about this place from my contact list. My soul was in danger. Block me from danger, Lord. Jesus said that snakes are shrewd. We must be shrewd yet innocent. (Matthew 10:16).

I pay attention to what I remember dreaming. If Joseph and the three wise men acted on revelations from dreams (Matthew 1:20; 2:12–13), why should I not consider messages in my dreams? Even Pilate's wife paid attention to what she dreamed and warned her husband not to have anything to do with that innocent man (Matthew 27:19). Then consider Genesis 28:1–18. While on the run for fear that his twin, Esau, would take his life, Jacob dreamed about a ladder that reached from earth to heaven. In the dream, God identified himself, and Jacob believed God. To develop the intimacy the Lord requires, we must pay attention to any means he chooses to communicate with us. We must be deliberate about moving beyond discipleship to relationship with Christ.

Block me from me, Lord. Block me from danger and disobedience. Block me from visiting places I should avoid. Block me from doing things I should not do. Block me from thinking things I should not think. Stop me from being judgmental because others are not where I think they should be in you. Help me to distinguish being judgmental from having the privilege of observing the fruit that others bear. Help me to be more concerned about what I produce for you, Lord.

Personal Points to Ponder

Sit back and allow the Lord to show you yourself. Then fill in the blanks.

Lord, block me from:

Protect me from:

Make your steps firm. When you stumble, you will not fall. (Psalm 37:23–24).

Temple Maintenance: Be a Body Builder

Decide to abide in the Lord and maintain your temple. When you make a daily effort to abide in the Lord, you begin to grow in intimacy with him. Intimacy helps you to understand the Word of God in ways you never considered before. For example, I once attended at workshop at which the facilitator reminded us that the Spirit of God does not live in "substandard housing." That made me rethink my health and nutrition practices, especially my eating habits. What foods and medicines was I unnecessarily ingesting while expecting the Lord to live in me?

You must take an all-inclusive approach to caring for yourself and maintain your physical, emotional, and spiritual well-being to be the most effective instrument possible. I have decided to maintain the body God loaned me so that he can live in it and use me in his service. I do not want the Lord to post a sign on me that reads "Condemned" or "Vacancy." The healthier I am mentally and physically, the more I can be used to build up the body of believers. I must help equip the saints recognizing that I am being built so that God can dwell in me. (Ephesians 2:19–22). I must keep myself in check and guard against high cholesterol, obesity, hypertension, and diabetes. I cannot control everything, but I do not have to eat my favorite foods all the time. I watch the portions on my plate and exercise regularly.

I do these things as a form of worship. I offer my body back to God as a living sacrifice. (Romans 12:1). The healthier I remain, the more intense my praise and worship become. Every movement is to God, for God, because of God. I must maintain his temple so he does not have to vacate substandard housing.

Our bodies are God's temples (1 Corinthians 3:16–17; 6:19–20; 2 Corinthians 6:16; Acts 7:48; 17:24). God does not live in man-made temples. (Acts 17:24). We are not rocks, and the buildings in which we worship are not the church. We are the church. God works in us to act accordingly. (Philippians 2:13, Ephesians 1:5, 9; 2:19). We are here for his will according to his pleasure, which he purposed in Christ. Anything we do should be purposed in him because he is in us.

I am flesh and blood. In God, I live, move, and have my being. Jesus said if the people remain silent the stones will cry out. (Luke 19:40). The multitude of people had thrown their clothes in the way when Jesus was descending the Mount of Olives the week before he was crucified. They loudly rejoiced, praising God for the mighty works they had seen. Luke 19:36–39 notes that after they blessed Jesus, some of the Pharisees told him to rebuke or censure them. They wanted Jesus to show disapproval of their praise. Jesus responded that if they held their tongues, the stones would immediately cry out. He approved of the loud voices honoring him and acknowledged that this had to happen.

While we are alive, we have Jesus' approval to praise him with the words coming out of our mouths. He is not saying the rocks will cry out in our place; the rocks are not our substitutes, nor will Jesus reside in them. He is saying that even a rock has sense enough to know who Jesus is. If we do not praise him, that is on us. Our failure to rejoice in the Lord will not prevent another's praise. One way or another, Jesus will be recognized as King, and no one can stop the praise. Man was created for God's glory (Isaiah 43:7), so we must glorify him; we must offer him a sacrifice of praise while in these earthly temples. Upon this rock Jesus will build his church (Matthew 16:18). We are the church, and no one can stop us from being that unless we allow it. We are responsible for maintaining our temples, and the decision to do that is ours alone.

After publicly accepting my call to ministry, I realized that my biggest opponent was myself. I had convinced myself that I was not up to the task, though I did not know what I was telling myself I could not do. I let others decide who I ought to be, what I ought to do, and how I ought to do it. Without realizing it, I tried to live up to others' expectations and harmed my position with Christ. Doing this also hindered my ability to maintain my temple. Who does not look back and see things he or she would do differently? The restrictions I placed on myself were an attempt to rationalize my failure to submit to the call. I was my greatest opponent, an obstacle I had to overcome. I would look at a hurdle and touch it, but would not try to jump over it. My initial rejection of the call and later hesitation in accepting it were self-inflicted wounds. Block me from me.

The apostle Paul said there were good things he would do, but the conflict within his flesh had him do otherwise (Romans 7:14–24). When evil is in the presence of the Lord, it must flee. I pray that the Lord will help me avoid people who seek to destroy my relationship with him. Sometimes we encounter people who intentionally try to take our attention away from godly things. If we stand on our faith, abide in the Lord, and confront the conflict, we experience victory in Jesus. The Lord who is in you can overpower the enemy every time. Decide to abide in the Lord and maintain your temple.

Personal Point to Ponder

Journal your thoughts and feelings now.

Barbara A. F. Brehon

Soar above your world and ask God what he is up to in your life.

"Another Mountaintop Experience"
over the Swiss Alps, November 2004

Connect with Christ

> I want to know Jesus. I want his power. I want to fellowship
> with him even through the good and the bad. I choose
> to be connected with Christ. (Philippians 3:10).

There are many kinds of connections. You can be connected to something or with something. You can connect to airline flights and to fuel lines. You can connect to power sources that make life so much easier than it was long ago. Using a cell phone, you can be connected in conversation with persons hundreds of miles away while driving in your car, walking through a mall, or sitting in your living room. You hear the voice of someone on the other side of the globe. Tablets and apps connect you quickly with anybody anywhere in the world. Technological connections allow you to access all kinds of information in cyberspace. However, none of these connections is as important as the one God expects us to have with him through his Son, Jesus.

In Philippians 3:5, the apostle Paul connects himself with his heritage. He speaks of his circumcision, being from the tribe of Benjamin, being a Hebrew, and being a Pharisee. Heritage is important; it has value. But it is nothing without a connection with Christ. Paul had connections to the church at Philippi. In Philippians 1:1–8 we learn that he rejoiced when remembering fellowship with the saints in Philippi in the gospel. He affectionately recalled them as partakers of grace with him. In Philippians 4:15 we find that the Philippian church was the only one that gave to Paul's early ministry when he left Macedonia. Philippi was the capital of this province, and it had a rich history dating back to Alexander the Great. It was now a Roman colony (Acts 6:12), actually more like a miniature Rome, yet Paul was able to establish the first church in Europe there. He connected himself with his heritage and with the people sharing God's grace. Paul realized that he was a body builder for the Lord, and he demonstrated that he cared deeply about those people.

Heritage is important. I remember my great-grandmother, Lucie Litchfield Wilson, quietly sitting in a rocking chair beside the picture window at my grandmother's house. She died at 103. She had been a slave who was emancipated in 1863 at age six. She was responsible for starching and pressing the linen for the communion table at First Baptist Church on Bute Street in Norfolk, Virginia, the oldest black church in the city.

Yes, heritage is important; it is important for us to know our connections. I am connected with Richard and Jerlean because they were my parents. I am connected with Nita, Dickie, Don, and Tony because they are my siblings. I am connected with Norfolk because I was born, raised, and made my living there. I am connected with organizations in the community, the state, and the nation. But all this is rubbish if I am not connected with Christ. If we are able to remember our heritage in the world, why should we not remember our heritage in Christ? I choose to be connected with Christ.

We must evaluate our lives to determine what is important. What matters most is to know Christ. Christians who want a closer relationship with God must know the power of Jesus' resurrection. Growing disciples must embrace the fellowship of his sufferings. What really matters is to be conformed to his death.

To Know Christ

You must honestly answer this question: do you want to know Jesus? If the answer is yes, then spend time getting to know your Savior and make him your top priority. Your days and weeks may get hectic, but do not edge him out of your life. Decide each day to abide in Him. You make time for everything you want, and you must make time to connect with Christ daily.

Jesus must be more than a casual acquaintance. I know somebody who knows Joe, so I know about Joe. But knowing Jesus must be more personal than knowing about him through someone else. Knowing Jesus means learning from your encounters with him. This involves more than knowing facts or doctrine about Jesus and implies more than a loose connection. You must know Jesus well enough so you can comfortably introduce him to somebody else. To know him is to feel, to perceive, and to understand a being who is beyond yourself but who abides within you. You cannot discern him with your senses, but you know him to be real. I know that Jesus is the Son of God. You must be found in Christ and have righteousness through faith in Christ to know him.

Paul said he did not want to have his own righteousness. He wanted righteousness from God by faith. (Philippians 3:9). Righteousness is the establishment of a right relationship with God. Righteousness has everything to do with justification, the judicial act of God. You can be made right with God only by God, who grants unmerited pardon from sin when you profess faith in Jesus Christ as his Son. The object of justification is that you may know Christ, especially in connection with his resurrection. Righteousness cannot be attained based on what you do; the wicked think like that. Righteousness is a gift from God; it is available only through Jesus Christ. Oh, that I may be fully acquainted with his nature, his character, his work. The highest object of desire for the Christian ought to be to know Christ.

1 John 3:2 lets us know that we will be like Christ when he is revealed. To see God, you must be in communion with him. To know him is to commune with him. This knowledge is not gained by hearing or by reading but by making time to be with God. When you do this, your sharing about your relationship with the Lord is sweeter to those who hear you. Some will reject what you say. They are not rejecting you but the Spirit they witness in you. Your time with the Lord will yield an unmistakable sincerity as you walk through life. The lack thereof is equally revealing; not knowing him shows.

To Know the Power of His Resurrection

The power is God's strength. Paul stressed the inherent power of the resurrection of Jesus. This power resides in us and makes itself known in the effort of choosing to believe. I do not mean to make this sound easy; we may have to make sacrifices. Jesus sacrificed his life to be resurrected. Offering our bodies is a means of worshiping the Lord (Romans 12:1). To fully enjoy the power that can be ours when we are connected with

Christ, we may have to sacrifice something: friends, family, or freedom. This does not mean freedom as we know it, for true freedom liberates the soul. Freedom is never free; someone pays for it. A liberated soul is what matters; it is the essence of who we are, not what we pretend to be for the sake of others' expectations. God wants to set us free. We must let him enter that most private and intimate place in our hearts.

God wants us to know him through his saving Son. When we know him like that, we may lose other relationships. But according to Philippians 3:8, anything but Jesus ought to be counted as dung, as in the excrement of animals, worthless and detestable. We must count all else as rubbish for the cause of the gospel of Christ Jesus. What about the plans, pleasures, and approval-seeking activities that crowd our calendars? Dung! We must keep what connects us with Christ on the calendar if we want eternal life.

"Resurrection"
Church of the Ascension, Holy Land, 2003
No one sees exactly what you see. "Don't take the picture like that; the sun will be in it." How beautiful to see in print what I saw then.

If we connected ourselves to Jesus in all aspects of our lives, his influence would raise our minds above the world. We would be better able to deal with our suffering until we are resurrected or raptured. No truth

Beyond Discipleship to Relationship

has greater power than the truth that Christ has risen from the dead. Great God from Zion! His resurrection makes it certain that there is a future, the dead will also rise. Christ's resurrection dispels the darkness around the grave. Full belief in the fact that Jesus has risen from the dead produces a sure hope that we also shall be raised. This belief helps us to bear trials for his sake, with the assurance that we shall be raised up as he was. That truth bonds us with him and with others in the world.

To Know the Fellowship of His Sufferings

To think of suffering as fellowship is awesome and mind-boggling. When we are in fellowship, we choose to be in union with something or someone. Being physically present is not fellowship. Fellowship means binding together to make an alliance. Fellowship cannot be forced. Early Christians decided that they wanted to be in association, in communion, sharing what they had. (Acts 2:42 NKJV).This suggests spiritual intimacy, fellowship, and communication. We fellowship with companions in Christ our Savior.

To know the power of the resurrection, we must share Jesus' sufferings. He has borne our grief and carried our sorrow. Our sufferings must be united with the sufferings of Jesus. Paul wished to be identified with him, to be just like his Savior. Everything that Christ did was glorious in Paul's view, and he wished in all things to resemble Jesus. Paul did not desire merely to share Jesus' honors and triumphs in heaven, but wished to be wholly conformed to the Lord's glorious work, to be just like Christ. He counted it an honor to be permitted to suffer as Jesus did. The true Christian will esteem it a privilege to be made just like him, not only in glory, but also in trial. Are we seeking merely the honors of heaven, or do we consider it a privilege to be reproached and reviled as Christ was?

To Be Conformed to His Death

We must become like Jesus in his death; Paul would have rejoiced to go to the cross like Jesus and die in the same way, enduring scorn and pain. Today conformity to Christ's death is measured by the depth of our obedience from the inside out. Becoming like Jesus in his death means daily dying to self and denying our own agendas to live holy lives. Self-righteousness dies when we choose the ways of Jesus. If we conform to his death, we choose to receive the same form as Christ unto death. We must be crucified with him. (Galatians 2:20).

What matters most is the resurrection from the dead. When we get to heaven, what a day of rejoicing that will be! When we see Jesus, we will sing and shout the victory. Every sacrifice made on earth is a milestone on the way to that victory. The question is, how much are we willing to sacrifice and to exert ourselves to be just like Jesus? Only when believers in Christ come to know his resurrection power can they fellowship with him in sufferings and die to sin and to self.

What really matters? What matters is to know Jesus and the power of his resurrection. It matters to be in fellowship with his sufferings. What matters is to be conformed to his death in order to be raised from the dead.

Personal Points to Ponder

Answer each question that follows to evaluate yourself. Write the response that immediately comes to mind, and be honest with yourself.

- Am I willing to suffer with Christ as well as to reign with him?

- Am I willing to wear a crown of thorns as well as a crown of glory?

- Am I willing to put on a robe of contempt on earth as well as a robe of splendor in heaven?

- Am I willing to share the poverty and persecution of redemption as well as the triumphs?

Tough times never last, but tough people do. (a thought from my Uncle Jimmy)

PART 2

Build Relationships
Get a Grip
Biblical Paradigms

"The Savior of Men"
Carved and photographed by Gregory Brehon, October 2013. Used with permission.
We can see Jesus in anything if we look hard enough. Intimacy
helps us to see him, not find him because he is not lost; we are.

Build Relationships

The people of God must above all be spiritually stable and continue to grow. The curriculum counts for nothing if it is not fully rooted in the Bible. Human beings, created in God's image for his good pleasure, matter most. If you want to move beyond discipleship to a more intimate relationship with Christ, you must ensure that materials you read, including this book, align with the Word of God. Christian educators must be concerned with developing people for God, using whatever material the Holy Spirit provides to build them up. Hold your leaders accountable for feeding you with all the depth and the richness you can digest. The Bible says that followers of Christ must be body builders equipping the saints (Ephesians 2:19–22). This must happen at every spiritual level.

To grow closer to the Savior, turn to the gospel story for insight on how to be in relationship. The four gospel writers reveal the truth to the spiritually discerning. With modern technology at your fingertips, you can listen to an entire book of the Bible in minutes. If you are wondering what to do about a problem, read the gospels all the way through to get a clear picture of what Jesus said and did in various circumstances. Then imitate him. What power! This place in the Lord is so sweet, I do not want to leave it. But I know how to return. The Word is ever available. The Holy Spirit can bring me back. Jesus intercedes for me before the Father, presenting me to him. Wow! How breathtaking is that—to be in such relationship that you feel favored by the Father?

Tap into the Power Source

People in our congregations come from all walks of life. Ushering them through spiritual processes is challenging, since each congregant has a unique set of assumptions, values, and priorities. These differences lead to a variety of perceptions about church matters, especially the preaching, teaching, and music ministries. Perception is relevant to a believer's ability to apply biblical lessons learned. Consider times when you questioned something that was said or done. You meant no harm; you simply wanted to know the truth. There are people sitting in your church now doing the same thing in regard to some point or another. Though this subject should not be an issue, it has captured the attention of congregants, taking the focus from the Father. The difference of opinion is not necessarily a bad thing, but it has become a distraction to the mission.

Collaborative efforts (using triads, or partnerships of three) in a congregation would enable believers, Christ's companions, to perceive and wrestle with perceptions before and during application of the principles being taught. Church members must desire to cultivate a relationship with Christ and to share that relationship with others. Once they have made that decision, they can be escorted through a developmental process. As new disciples grow and seasoned congregation members develop discipling skills, ministries must be in place to take advantage of the many gifts these people will bring.

The church is flesh and blood and as such is a social melting pot. Christians are social beings just like individuals who have not yet decided to follow Christ. That makes a congregation's social setting important. The church must make available members who can reach others through common experiences in the community or in the workplace. Did you first decide to follow Jesus while you were in a church sanctuary, in a concert crowd, or during an intimate talk with one or two other believers?

Churches can easily embrace partnerships as intimate opportunities for sharing encounters with Christ. People in these partnerships can contribute knowledge, skills, and experiences they have had with Christ in daily circumstances. Teams of partners may function in different ways, depending on the needs that arise and the time that schedules allow. Faithful followers of Christ tapping into the power source sometimes need help discerning what is of God or what is a trick of the enemy. Believers must seek seasoned saints to escort them along their journey. Each mile of the way may call for a different type of seasoning. Ask God to show you whom he wants you to partner with on this journey.

Barbara A. F. Brehon

The Best Ministry Approach

Members of the church, who are Christ's disciples and represent many disciplines within society, come together for the benefit of the congregation. Keep in mind why you are a member, recalling the early church described in the book of Acts. Disciples become involved in the growth of others while growing themselves. Daily struggles do not deter them from pursuing change and becoming more Christ-like. Morning by morning new mercies I see; therefore, I cannot ever feel like I graduate from growing.

The discipleship deficit can be changed to a surplus when people are provided settings conducive to intimate nurture. The Bible is the instruction book, and the church is the base for every disciple-making strategy. Obeying the Great Commission to make disciples means more than winning souls. Once a soul is won it must be nurtured. The new disciple needs a structure that offers a strong sense of belonging. Along with this, skilled persons who practice the faith in daily life and are trained by the Holy Spirit must befriend others and build healthy relationships.

There is potential for competition and conflict among church members, but true disciples are most concerned about being productive for the kingdom. God created people for his glory and to be connected with one another, and this fact says a great deal about healthy relationships. The best example is Jesus. As a child, he grew. Even while growing up he pleased God and men. (Luke 2:52). A congregation contains quite a mix of people who can be used to help others develop more intimate relationships with Christ through triads within the church. You will not share the details of your life with anyone who will listen. You need confidants along the way, and others need you to help them get through the situations you have already faced.

Imagine being a social worker who is handling relationships. Some associations are brief encounters while others are ongoing. A triad in the kingdom of God need not be perpetual. People enter our lives for a season. Persons whom I mentor in my congregation have identified their spiritual gifts, developed and deployed them, learned that the gifts were best suited for a certain ministry, and have been empowered to use those gifts in new relationships. When you consider where you are compared with where you used to be, you will see that you have grown through relationships. God impels you to move in Christ; you do not have to be confined in a box. You must hold yourself accountable and provide opportunities for spiritual growth. These may not look like anything you have ever tried before.

The people I have mentored advanced in spiritual maturity by sharing with others focused on growing in Christ. No one grows without help. Moreover, with this growth model people are willing to replicate the process for others because the experiences were effective for them. As a spiritual nurturer, I do not ignore those moving to other ministries. I coach them in their new environment to persevere through the trials of change. I encourage them to remain focused on the Father, using their gifts for God, not man.

Collaborative relationships are built on mutual respect and positive communication. Mature Christians help others by seeing needs rather than faults. Persons in relationships must continually recognize that people view different things as important. Collaborative or mentoring relationships must keep that in mind. Spiritual mentors must recognize when more or less of a particular approach is needed. Different levels of assertiveness and cooperation can yield compromise, avoidance, competition, or accommodation. Mentors must exercise spiritual discernment to determine what to do and when to do it. The purpose is growth, and they must keep focused on that goal while enjoying the work and the fellowship. Others may not always agree, but nurturers should not be disagreeable. They must value diversity.

The church is a social melting pot. Recognizing this empowers, stimulates creativity, promotes teamwork, learning, and comfort with implementing change, motivates increased responsibility with accountability, develops potential, enables open and direct communication, and fosters collaboration among peers in all age groups. Christian nurturers not only want disciples to grow, but to create opportunities for growth within a sound setting. That could be any ministry, committee, or subcommittee in the church.

Inside Relationships

Collaboration, mentoring, partnering, and coaching are most effective in an environment that supports these things. Effective small groups functioning within larger church organizations depend on receptive leadership and a congregation's willingness to follow the leadership through a spiritual growth process. The process must embrace church ministries and a teaching style that facilitates Christian growth. Small teams within ministries should rely on a variety of healthy spiritual relationships.

We must also realize that although they mean well, significant others, accountability partners, and nurturers are not always right about spiritual matters. Each disciple must depend on an individual relationship with God. When we see Jesus face to face, we will be standing on our own relationship. We must grow it now while there is still time. We must go to the Father through the Son, Jesus the Christ, led by the sweet Holy Spirit. Ah, the blessed Trinity—so sweet!

Several experiences have shown me the sweetness of intimacy with the Lord. Before I began revisions to this book, the leading of the Holy Spirit prompted me to determine how my writing had evolved by listing my publications in chronological order. (See "More from the Author.") In doing that, I could see clear seasons for my writing. I could also see my ministry focus, the call to do specific works for the Lord. I saw that what I do in ministry and what I write for publications have remained one and the same. Whatever I do and wherever I go, I must follow my call rather than someone else's expectations. I must not allow distractions (what other people think I should be doing) to deter me from God's purpose for me.

Two months after one of these distractions, I attended a revival in my community. I sat in a pew with friends, but during the service the pastor invited me to the pulpit. This made the evangelist aware of me. We had not previously met. After the three of us finished greeting the congregation at the door following worship, the evangelist spoke prophetic words privately to me. His undeniable urgency could not have been premeditated. The Spirit of God in me received his message. The previous night I had encountered God's presence, which warned me to prepare for an event about to happen. I did not know what that would be, but I began to pray for clarity and obedience.

After returning home from the revival, I was sitting peacefully in my favorite chair, the same place I had been the night before, reflecting on the prophetic words spoken to me. The experience of the previous night repeated itself. Still not knowing God's intent, I found it exciting that he was acting for his good pleasure. I asked someone the next day to join me in prayer for my obedience to the Lord's will; I did not find it necessary to offer details. Intimacy with the Lord is sweet. Several weeks later, God gifted me with an enormous blessing. There are blessings in obedience (Deuteronomy 28:3–6). I know that he blessed me so that I can be a blessing to someone else.

What a blessing it is to know that you are on the right course and to get confirmations or warnings from God. The Lord will alert you when you are about to suffer an attack by the enemy. God communicates warnings so you can be prepared for every attack. He will provide the protection and the resources you need to keep focused on working for him.

The Lord formed an impromptu triad (the pastor, the evangelist, and myself) with lasting results even though I may never have another encounter with that evangelist/prophet. He said he discerned that I knew how to be quiet and warned me to be cautious in a particular matter that I had not divulged to him. Another minister whom I know well was there but had to leave early and was not at the door with us. God's will, God's way, every step along the way. One more preacher at the back door may have distracted me from receiving what God prepared for me that night.

Distractions are harmful to God's plans, and I must choose what enhances and complements my work for the Lord. The enemy uses distractions to stop Christians from fulfilling their purpose in the Lord. I must be aware of how I let others influence my life. They may mean well, but my relationship with the Lord must be intimate enough that I know his voice and his will. I must hear from the Lord first. Then others may confirm what God has revealed. I am leery of those speaking a word to me that the Lord did not put in my spirit before hearing it from them. I am courteous but cautious. God may be using these voices to sharpen my recognition of his voice. Intimacy with the Savior is sweet.

Personal Points to Ponder

Consider your relationships and identify them. List or describe who is in that intimate circle with you.
Family:
Work:

Church:

Community:

Other:

Refer to the list you just made. Whom would you consider an enhancement or a distraction to your work for God? You might want to circle or highlight the enhancers. They are your wheat. Pray for God's guidance about the others, your tares. (Read Matthew 13:24–30 for descriptions of wheat and tares.)

Get a Grip

Hold on to things you have learned from the Scriptures so that
you will not be deceived by anyone. 2 Thessalonians 2:3, 15

The second chapter of 2 Thessalonians concerns the second coming of Christ. I implore you to preserve your soul for Christ's return. When you are at your weakest, or when things are going well and you are not spiritually alert, the wheat and the tares will tell you all kinds of things. Keep your balance—wheat on one side, tares on the other, the Lord as the balance beam.

Verse 15 recommends getting a grip on traditions taught through words and actions. Get a grip on who God is in your life, and keep that footing firm because false teachers will try to fool you. Have you ever grabbed on to something? Getting a grip on an object is different from holding it or having it. To hold on to God, you need balance.

A balance scale has a beam in the center with two pans suspended at opposite sides. You put objects on both sides to judge any difference in weight. You add or take away from one side to create balance. Weights are imprinted with their amounts. You use the weight that you judge to most closely fit what you are measuring. As a Christian, you are imprinted with Christ. Is your imprint accurate?

If you were a little shady, you would use a mislabeled weight. The weight might say five pounds when you know it's only four. If you were measuring out grain, you would get more money for less product. A false balance does not delight God, and 2 Thessalonians 2:12 warns that those who don't believe the truth and enjoy wickedness will be condemned. The spiritual weights we use must be accurately marked. Honesty is from the Lord. (Proverbs 16:11). But how do you get a grip on God and keep it? You must remember the three i's: integrity, identity, and intelligence.

Barbara A. F. Brehon

Christian Integrity

You must always have integrity. That's honesty, uprightness, and reliability. A just weight can be depended on for accuracy. You must also keep a just balance. You must possess poise and stability. Your equilibrium must be centered in Christ, your balance beam. Remember your Christian teachings. Walk with integrity. When you call yourself a Christian, family and friends are watching to see how you measure up.

Don't pretend to be something you are not. Your relationship with the Lord is what it is. You should not overemphasize loving the Lord to the point of being phony. The ones closest to you discern your sincerity. The Lord does not like dishonesty. (Proverbs 20:23).You must rely on a steady standard: the Bible, with its account of the life of Christ. To use any other standard is disgusting to God. Have you ever been disgusted? Would you want God to feel that way about you? Do what you must to bring him delight. Don't delight in wickedness. Get a grip on God, then keep that grip.

Christians must weigh their thoughts and actions; that's Christian integrity. Weigh them so that you stay focused on pleasing the Lord rather than having to correct yourself or apologize later. You must be aware of the balance between God and yourself. Are you measuring up to his standard? You certainly cannot measure him against yourself. It's you who must measure up. Balanced against the blessings God has given you, how do you measure up? You will find God's favor if you give him credit for what is in your bag of weights and measures.

Christian Identity

You need to know your identity. Know who you are. Know that you are called to salvation. (2 Thessalonians 2:14). God has done so much for you, and you must offer righteousness in return. You must be holy. (Leviticus 19:35–36). Don't be dishonest even with yourself. Get a grip on God and your identity, then keep that grip. Do what is right because it is right.

Job wanted his grief and his calamity to be measured. (Job 6:2). He wanted to create a balance between what happened to him and how he felt

Beyond Discipleship to Relationship

about it. You must create a balance between what grieves you (what could destroy you) and how you feel about it (your anger or bitterness). That's part of getting a grip. Know what you are, know why you are, and know how you are. That's identity.

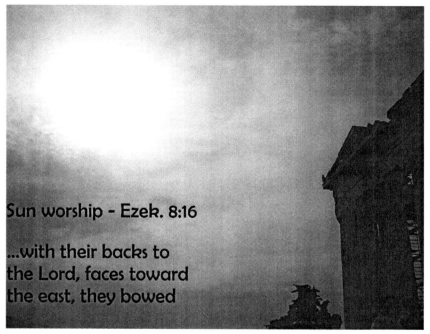

"Who Made the Sun?"
Greece, November 2004

Christian Intelligence

Do not lose sight of who God is in your life. You are supposed to share in the glory of Jesus Christ. Don't be duped! Paul warned believers not to become worried or troubled by what people say about Jesus' return. (2 Thessalonians 2:2–3). Use your intelligence, and make sure that what people are telling you aligns with the Lord. If you're not sure, ask God, "What do you think? Is this you, Lord? Is this your will? Or is this person trying to fool me?"

Just as you don't want to be deceived, you must not be the deceitful one. Christians must delight the Lord, not disgust Him. Creating a false balance disgusts God. (Proverbs 11:1). Remember that Christ chose to stay on that old rugged cross for your sin and mine. Remember his suffering. Remember his blood. Remember his beaten body. Remember his death. But most of all, remember his resurrection so that you can get a grip on God and keep it.

Personal Points to Ponder

As you reflect on what you have been gripping, consider where you need more balance.
Family:
Work:
Church:
Community:
Other:

Biblical Paradigms

The concept of moving beyond discipleship to disciple-making and a more intimate relationship with the Lord is founded on a biblical pattern derived from two verses. The first is taken from a portion of the Great Commission, Matthew 28:19. In John 15:8, Jesus says we must bear much fruit.

Both gospels, Matthew and John, were written for the church and depict the struggles of Christian communities. The two books are attributed to the persons whose names they bear. Matthew wrote about signs that Jesus performed in the presence of his disciples so that we would believe Jesus is the Christ. By believing that Jesus is the Son of God we gain eternal life (John 20:30–31). The writings of John reflect the tensions between community and the interpretation of Jesus.[4]

In addition to these paradigms or examples, we will look at what comprises a vision within a body of believers that bears fruit. We will also explore several biblical triads, or groups of three, that provide a foundation for moving beyond discipleship to a more intimate relationship with Christ.

According to Matthew

The gospel of Matthew illustrates the concept of moving beyond discipleship to disciple-making and a more intimate relationship with the Lord. It recounts how Jesus recruited Matthew, a tax collector, to be his disciple (Matthew 9:9–10). Matthew had done his work as a tax collector in public, which suggests his booth was in the middle of town. The community knew him before he met Jesus. His new life as a disciple required that he extend the opportunity for others to know Christ. After deciding to follow Jesus, not only did Matthew invite the Lord to his house but he asked his publican colleagues to join them. One can conclude that Matthew wanted his associates to become more intimately acquainted with Jesus.

As the Messiah, Jesus offers the kingdom of God to the people who believe in him. Today new converts and seasoned Christians coexist with publicans as in the time of Matthew. There is a daily struggle to live according to the standards of one's belief system whether it embraces Christ or not. Both the believer in Jesus as Messiah and the nonbeliever face opposition from those with alternative views and lifestyles. People must decide daily whether to follow the standards of the community or the teachings of the Christ. Matthew set the example of choosing to follow Jesus and inviting others to investigate the Lord for themselves. His fellowship with others was his opportunity to bear witness to his growing relationship with Jesus.

The gospel of Matthew is concerned with how persons live in relationship with Jesus as well as with one another. Among the gospel writers, only Matthew uses the term *church* and the phrase *make disciples* (16:18; 18:17; 28:19).

When he told his followers to make disciples, Jesus took them a step beyond what they had been doing. The Lord's listeners had been students of his teachings; they had listened to him and had practiced what they had learned. Jesus had been with them and available for them to share their concerns when they faced frustrating or confusing situations. Jesus was their escort through a growth process that produced more disciples. He wanted the disciples to continue to practice what they had learned. He wanted them to go beyond where they had been. Disciple-making is a step beyond discipleship to a more intimate relationship with the Lord.

According to Matthew, when Jesus spoke to his disciples before his ascension, he was on a mountain in Galilee, as Moses had been on Mount Sinai. Jesus was the fulfillment of the Old Testament, and this account would make the Jewish Christians of Matthew's time more accepting of the Christ event. Jesus commissioned the disciples to expand their witnessing efforts to include the Gentiles, since a relationship with God is not based on race. By doing so, Jesus rescinded his earlier commissioning of the disciples, which excluded the Gentiles (Matthew 10:5). The mission of making disciples would now be motivated by the desire to offer a personal relationship with God to all. Proof of the Christ event would lie in the testimony of the witnesses and in the growth of the church as the witnesses went forth.

Personal Points to Ponder

How do you use relationships to share your faith? Explain by noting what steps you take.

According to John

The relationship of John to Jesus can teach the church a great deal about ministry. The organized church is a community of believers in Jesus Christ as the Son of God. However, believers struggle with tradition as it relates to doing ministry and teaching in the church. As an eyewitness to the glory of Christ, John was present with Jesus, sharing intimate times. (John 1:14).

John was the disciple whom Jesus loved (John 21:20). He was the one who leaned on Jesus' breast at the Last Supper. John saw the crucifixion (John 19:35). Intimate experiences similar to those in John's relationship with Jesus are possible today. The church can create a climate that provides opportunities for individuals to develop relationships while remaining connected to Christ.

John says that Jesus is the vine and that his disciples are the branches (John 15:5). He wants us to know who Jesus is so we can choose a new way of life that leads to eternity. Chapters 14 and 15 provide an allegory linking Christ to his church as a vine is connected to its branches. Because of this link, believers will be able to do great things, bearing much fruit. The teachings of Jesus prune his disciples in preparation for fruit bearing. There are hundreds of references to fruit and fruitfulness in the Bible.

The invisible power of the Holy Spirit in those who are brought into living union with Christ (John 15:2–8) produces the fruit of the Spirit (Galatians 5:22). This union compels the disciple to action. According to the *Dictionary of Biblical Imagery*, fruit, as used in this verse, is the result of an action.[5] Fruit can be rendered good or bad. The righteous person demonstrates fruitfulness, whereas unfruitfulness strangles spiritual life and vigor. Fruitfulness represents a benefit to others. The unfruitful person is not productive, doing nothing and yielding nothing. Fruit is the proof of discipleship. Until believers have borne fruit, they do not deserve to be called disciples. Persons who hear about the Christ event are forced to respond to what they have heard; they will either believe or not believe. The commission of disciples is to share their experience of Christ with others. We see this in all the gospel narratives.

The Great Commission According to Matthew, Mark, Luke, and John

Refer to Matthew 28:18–20, Mark 16:15–18, Luke 24:47–53, John 20:21–23 and compare the Great Commission according to each gospel writer.

Results are expected of the disciple, but they come from a connection to the vine.[6] The vine generates the fruit. Yet there is clearly an element of personal responsibility involved in this. By abiding in Christ, the disciple depends on him, sees the importance of Scripture, and recognizes a responsibility to pray and the need to grow further.

Religion is not as important to our society as it was in Jesus' time. Therefore Christians must imitate the Lord and take an interest in the daily relationships of those whom they disciple. Jesus spoke to the multitudes, but he also spent much time in intimate situations with small groups or with just one person. These people were the ones who testified about their experiences with him. Among those encountering the Lord in this way were Nicodemus, the woman at the well, Mary, Martha, Lazarus, and the disciples in the garden. In chapter 3, John cites Nicodemus as seeking Jesus, and in 19:38–40 the evangelist reports that this disciple used a hundred pounds of myrrh and aloes to prepare Jesus' body for burial, then bound it with linen strips. Disciples offer witness in what they do as well as in what they say. Personal witness moves believers to build relationships with God through Jesus Christ. We need not be religious; we must be saved.

John 15:8 provides further proof that disciple-making is a step beyond discipleship toward relationship with Christ. Jesus and his disciples were in the upper room where he taught them prior to his arrest. He identified true disciples as those who bear much fruit. To bear fruit is synonymous with discipling another person. The term *disciple* means a learner or a pupil. This verse goes a step further. Those who reveal themselves as disciples to others produce much fruit. But if there is no visible evidence that the learner has been taught, is the person a disciple? I am reminded of the comparison between fruit-bearing wheat and unproductive tares (Matthew 13:24–30).

Jesus said the evidence confirming discipleship is another disciple. John helps us accept responsibility for being productive disciples and tells us that we must show tangible evidence that we are what we claim.

In John 15:7, the evangelist uses the allegory of a vine to describe the relationship of a disciple, or learner, with a teacher. The vine represents the connection among the Father, Jesus, and the disciples. Staying connected to Jesus enables the disciple to be productive, thereby honoring God. "The branches of a vine are not self-centered or independent … Unwillingness … to draw from Jesus or to submit to the discipline which alone makes possible the flow of this vitalizing power, renders the so-called believer a dead branch unable to bear fruit."[7] Believers who want to be Christ's disciples must submit to being taught.

Discipleship is conditional. Jesus tells his disciples to remain in him. He also tells them that his words, which are commandments and doctrine, should continue to be in them. By remaining in Jesus and in his words, disciples regulate their lives.

God is honored when Jesus' disciples produce good works and are faithful to him. A disciple must resist the tendency to be religious and work in the church for the Lord's sake, not out of habit or tradition. A disciple must do good works, using energy, time, and resources for the church's mission to glorify God in the name of Jesus. Others see God's reflection in what an individual does and the way it is done. For the disciple, this is a true test of character, and actions count far more than words. Jesus said those who bear much fruit are his disciples, and this standard determines whether a church member is a disciple. Obeying the command to bear much fruit means sharing the gospel and convincing others to accept it as truth.

As he concluded his earthly ministry, Jesus said that his followers must make disciples and that disciples bear much fruit. A person who has learned from a teacher bears fruit and replicates the teaching. Christians who accept Jesus as their personal Savior must be productive replicators of their faith. A church intent on making disciples is a church that fulfills the Great Commission.

Barbara A. F. Brehon

Personal Points to Ponder

In Matthew 7:15–20, Matthew 21:18–22, and Mark 11:12–26, read more about bearing fruit, and note what the Spirit of God is saying to you regarding yourself.

A Fruit-Bearing Vision

Disciple-makers nurture, comfort, and encourage those who are steadfast in the faith despite adversity. We must show compassion for others. Each Christian is the balm God has sent into the world. We must dress the wounds of the people so that they experience his love. By meeting people where they sit, we fulfill the Great Commission. Mature Christians can escort others into a perpetually growing relationship with the Lord of love.

God's truth must be taught so that people can clearly see the steps that Jesus took as the model disciple-maker. We must provide opportunities for believers at various spiritual levels to grow in relationship with Christ and with others. Our people need spiritual escorts to provide nourishment and to show them how the Word of God says we should grow. People learn differently, and we must teach using methods that address those differences. True disciples are part of the reproductive cycle that makes other disciples for Christ.

When disciples produce fruit, they witness to others about Jesus so that these people come to know him for themselves. They continue to follow Jesus' example and make themselves available to these new disciples, listening to their concerns and pointing them in a direction that leads them closer to God. The step from discipleship to relationship with Christ is not limited to the new disciple. For various reasons, some disciples have not grown into sharing their witness and need to be nurtured just as Jesus nurtured the disciples he called.

Before his ascension at a mountain in Galilee, Jesus commanded that his followers make disciples of all nations. By doing this, they would help the church of Christ to multiply. Jesus directed that they teach others what he had taught them so that all would obey his precepts. Effective discipleship is conditional; believers who want to be Christ's disciples must submit to being taught. Obeying this command also means sharing the gospel so that people will accept it as the truth.

Jesus told his disciples to lead their lives in a manner that would teach others the gospel and everything that he commanded. He gave this command to provide his disciples with a purpose after he ascended. Working toward that goal produces fruit; the more we share our faith, the more we grow. Jesus told his disciples that everybody in the world needed to hear the gospel, and the same is true today. We teach others to observe all the things that Jesus commanded.

The church at its best fulfills the Great Commission to teach the gospel of Jesus Christ. Without the Christ event there would be no Christian church. Christ's life, death, resurrection, and ascension are the focal point of the mission of the church. Jesus commanded that those who believe in him tell others about him.

A closer relationship with God requires a change within the self. This is accomplished through the testimony of others who believe in the redemptive power of Jesus, which rescues us from sin. When others see the presence of Christ in another person's life that they know, they are more likely to want the same transformation in their own lives. The intimacy of the triads (new disciple, disciple-maker, and coach) fosters relationships in which baby Christians can see faith in action up close and personally. Those who want a new beginning may be restored to God; they do not have to be alienated from him.

The believer's response to obey God is a continuous process. After becoming a disciple, a person should show some evidence of that decision in the fruit produced. Jesus taught that God is glorified when a disciple bears much fruit.

Being in relationship with fellow believers provides strength for the journey. For example, you are going about your day when a coworker or a family member brings a proposal or a request to your attention and tries to convince you it is the will of God. The Spirit in you rises up and you discern that this is not true. At times like these, you can pull strength from the Lord and be affirmed in your triads. When you can share in confidence experiences that affect your walk, you are strengthened. Jesus said that false prophets come like sheep but are ferocious. Recognize them by their fruit. (Matthew 7:15–20).

A lack of spirituality shows. Bear fruit or you will be like the fig tree in Matthew 21:19–21 (Mark 11:12–14, 20–21). Jesus had left Bethany and was hungry. When he saw a fig tree, he approached it to pick the fruit. When he found no figs, he said, "May no one ever eat fruit from you again." The next morning the disciples saw the tree withered from the roots.

You must not let your relationship with God wither. You must bear fruit rather than remain spiritually barren. Eventually withered and unproductive trees are cut down. Disciple- making moves a Christian beyond discipleship to a perpetually growing relationship with Christ. You must do whatever you have to do to get your spiritual house in order.

Personal Points to Ponder

In Matthew 12:33–36 and Luke 13:6–9, read more about good fruit. Be sure that you listen to what the Spirit of the Lord is saying about your situation in life. Journal your response.

Developing a closer walk with God is crucial. One way to do that is to seek help from a small number of people: prayer partners, intimate others, an inner circle, small teams, accountability partners, triads. The key thing is to have someone to call, a person interested in your spiritual benefit. The people with whom you choose to share your thoughts and emotions are important. God does not want you to bear every burden on your own.

If you are wondering how to reach spiritual maturity, consider Peter, James, and John. They were part of Jesus' inner circle, and the gospels treat them as such several times. Peter, James, and John were the members of Jesus' triad.

Biblical Triads

- Jesus proclaimed that he would be present when two or three come together in his name. (Matthew 18:19–20).
- When he was restoring a girl to life, Jesus called for his inner circle. Jesus did not let anyone follow him except Peter, James, and John when he went to the synagogue ruler's house to restore life to his

daughter (Matthew 9:18–19, 23–25; Mark 5:22–24, 35–43; Luke 8:40–56).

- Jesus was the third person in each triad when he sent the disciples out two by two (Mark 6:7, 11:1–2). That is how we are to minister to one another, with Jesus as a part of every team.
- We find Jesus with a triad when he was transfigured. (Mark 9:2, Matthew 17:1–14 and Luke 9:28–36.)
- Before Jesus was crucified, he prayed in Gethsemane, but he did not go through his difficult time alone. (Mark 14:33; Matthew 26:37).
- Mary Magdalene, Mary the mother of James, and Salome formed a triad during Christ's passion. (Mark 16:1). The Lord would not have us bear our darkest moments alone. There are times for solitude, but there are more often times when we must share with others of like faith. We find this biblical triad in sorrow at the foot of the cross with Jesus' mother. Matthew 27:55 speaks of women beholding the crucified Christ from afar and names three (Mary Magdalene, Mary the mother of James the less and of Joses, and the mother of the sons of Zebedee). Mark 15:40 also names three (Mary Magdalene, Mary the mother of James the less and of Joses, and Salome). John alone mentions the mother of Jesus in the group. It is not clear whether the sister of the mother of Jesus is Salome the mother of the sons of Zebedee or the wife of Clopas. In John 19:25 these women stood by the cross of Jesus. It is important to note that the believers in this small, intimate group were not alone; they supported one another.

Spiritual Mentoring and Leadership

"I want to help others grow."

Moving from discipleship to relationship is not a complex process. The church can make study opportunities and fellowship available to members as a routine part of its teaching ministry. Any member would be able to enroll in the classes and participate in the fellowships, which would be repeated at cyclical intervals during the church year. So this program would involve a short-term series of sessions beyond midweek Bible study.

A church member deciding to grow in relationship with God through Jesus Christ would be escorted on the journey by a partner, who would listen to the person's testimonies along the way. Thus, the member would build a relationship for spiritual mentoring with a more seasoned saint. The classes and fellowships would propel the member toward growth. Personal and transparent testimonies would defuse devilish devices and strengthen babes in Christ.

People are more likely to share intimate personal stories in small triads. When held in confidence, these life-altering events help others see that the Lord's handiwork is also available to them. Larger groups are more intimidating for babes, and they are less likely to feel comfortable and safe about sharing their testimony. Including this developmental element in a church's ministry will also motivate congregation members to assess their spiritual maturity more often. Growing will not end until the return of Christ Jesus.

The church must give people opportunities for developing their discipleship. Those opportunities should be available from the time they commit to becoming members of the congregation. Persons who have not made an outward commitment should also be able to participate in church ministries. Disciple-making ministry opportunities may include Tuesday, Wednesday, and/or Thursday Bible study, Sunday school, vacation Bible school, and advanced Bible classes. Each should have classes for children, youths, and adults and encourage participation in conferences, conventions and workshops in fellowship with sister churches throughout the year.

PART 3

Ministering to Growing Disciples
Discipling Dilemma
Merging Processes

"Return from the mountain top to be poured out for the Lord"
Greece, November 2004

Ministering to Growing Disciples

Consider your context, or where you are. The Lord has blessed me to have served urban and rural congregations, and I have found that people have the same problems and need a closer walk with Jesus. Whether a church has fewer than a hundred members or more than a thousand, the mandates of the Word of God do not change, nor does the call to obey God's precepts. Whether the congregation is multiracial or completely segregated, and regardless of the economic and social standing of the members, the demands are the same.

Jesus taught during a time of tremendous religious, social, and political tension, and some of the people he taught were "almost fanatically religious."[8] Judaism preserved the Old Testament faith, though competing groups of Jews—Pharisees, Sadducees, Essenes, and Zealots—represented differing views. Some Jews assimilated into the culture while others resisted. The New Testament church was multicultural.

Jesus lived, taught, died, rose from the dead, and ascended to reign at the right hand of God. His social reforms created enemies, yet he focused on individuals and their relationships with one another and with a loving God. He was executed by his enemies but arose from the dead on the third day when he commissioned his disciples to tell others the good news about himself. The truth of the gospel lies in the meaning of the Christ event in the lives of believers.

We may have to minister to active-duty military people or to retirees raising grandchildren. People may be consumed with budding careers or be returning to school to complete requirements for promotion. We must meet people where they are and help them to grow in relationship with God. This will allow them to make better decisions about their lives. We must adhere to the guidelines of our faith and bloom where we are planted.

By the example of their lives, mature Christians help others see that a relationship with Christ is not physical or financial. The relationship demands fellowship with others of like mind. If the connection is not yet strong enough, Christians might associate with people who pull them away from a decision to follow the Lord. Jesus said that anyone not with him was against him. (Luke 11:23). We do not want our initial sincerity to be compromised. Associating in triads (intimate spiritual partnerships of three) helps us to stay grounded, nurtured, strong, and prepared to share our faith with others. While we grow, we are obligated by our faith to share our faith, thus strengthening others who choose to grow in God's grace.

Several times I have been reminded that the "small country church" is not the same as the "city church." When I hear comments like that, the only thing I can do is remain focused on the work in front of me. As for the people saying such things, I pray for their strength, their involvement, their health, and their families and expect that God will grow them into a closer relationship with him through faith in Jesus Christ—whether in the city or in the country. I will let them know that God called me to serve his people and to keep the integrity of the Word.

Context and custom will present challenges at times. But I celebrate and treasure a rich history while not letting it dictate how I observe God's commands. How wonderful it is to embrace people where they are and how they are and to lovingly escort them to more intimacy with the Christ. Jesus ministered in the city and in the country. He ministered in the temple, in the marketplace, and along the roadside. I would rather get on with the business of doing what he told me to do with the wheat, letting him handle the tares.

I once listened to a country revivalist discuss the wheat and the tares. Using Matthew 13:24–30, he helped us to see how to handle the tares in the church. That parable instructs us to let the tares grow up with the wheat until the harvest. Given enough time, the wheat will produce fruit and the tares will be dormant. Faultfinders and excuse-makers cannot stop fruit-bearers from being productive. We must not give more attention to the tares in the minority and sacrifice the growth of saints who are trying to bud and bear fruit. I cannot be convinced that the country preacher's message is not also true for congregations in the city, and so I focus on the work of the ministry. The Father has asked me to help people strengthen their relationship with him. We must not be weeded out. Let's be used for God's good pleasure.

Beyond Discipleship to Relationship

Attrition

Ministering to growing disciples carries certain challenges, one of which is attrition. Many churches experience negative attrition rather than membership gain. Attrition is a slow wearing down or dying out. It is a natural part of congregational life, and all churches experience it at some time or another. Attrition occurs when members of the congregation die. Some relocate and leave the church. Others join the church without matriculating through classes for new members; they do not begin a growth process and get disheartened for various reasons. Some churches do not offer classes or fellowship opportunities for new members. Some people stop attending after coming to a few worship services, preferring a different format or style of music. Others may stay longer, then switch to a different congregation for all kinds of reasons.

New members are not necessarily new converts, but a church should feel obligated to have programs in place to meet the spiritual needs of people at varying levels of Christian maturity. We must consider the problem realistically. The best way to defeat negative attrition is by growing the church from the inside out.

Congregations sometimes plateau, making paradigm shifts a necessity. When growth plateaus, the levels of participation stop climbing. Picture a line graph that depicts membership data and involvement in your church's ministries. The line had been rising year after year, but at some point it began to drop. The line may eventually flatten across the years. The line graph will look like someone was climbing a mountain, then reached a plateau.

To begin another climb, you cannot stand on the plateau. You must make some kind of move. When the same numbers of people are leaving and joining a church, it is time to do something different. A growth in numbers does not necessarily reflect spiritual growth; nevertheless, a gradual decline in numbers implies that a church needs more disciple-makers. The people sitting in the pews must sense an urgency to share their faith in Christ with others outside the church door. After attracting persons from the community, the church can add fellowships and other opportunities for people to get together to talk about their lives in Christ.

The church must build up its members spiritually by a vibrant teaching ministry that shows them the urgency of sharing their faith outside the walls where they meet. The needs of the current membership must also be met. How does the church address attrition and member retention?

Churches must create opportunities that facilitate the development of people and feed their desire to grow. This approach makes member retention a priority. One way to address retention and growth is to rethink Bible study. Churches must keep the traditional midweek classes. But they do not attract everybody, and something else must be in place to nudge members into personal development as disciples and disciple-makers. That may mean departing from tradition. Sometimes attrition occurs because disciples are growing but not being fed an appropriate diet for spiritual health. They look elsewhere for morsels of bread and living water. When you are hungry, do you sit and wait for someone to decide to feed you? When you are hungry, do you wait for someone to bring a plate to your room?

Personal Points to Ponder

How should the church minister to you as you pursue a closer relationship with the Lord?

How should the church minister to others as they grow in their relationships with the Lord?

Discipling Dilemma

The ministry approach I propose addresses the discipling dilemma of nurturing members into active involvement in church ministries. It involves seven sessions over two months. The concept draws support from the first portion of the Great Commission (Matthew 28) and the allegory of branches being connected to the vine (John 8). The discipling dilemma is not so great when the church uses an approach that is practical and portable. By constantly applying what they learn, disciples remain connected and have adequate nourishment to grow.

Growth is nurtured when individuals are connected to the body of believers by healthy relationships. The discipling ideas that follow are intended to build Christian relationships within the church through experiences encountered by participants desiring to grow closer to God. The ministry approach presented here was developed in an urban congregation but has been used in other settings.

Here is a description of the process that moves a church member from discipleship to a more intimate relationship with the Lord.[9]

1. The process begins with a disciple-maker who effectively shares his or her faith. The disciple-maker continues to be equipped while engaging others who enter into this process.
2. When a person who has been affected by the disciple-maker becomes a believer in Jesus Christ as his or her personal Savior, this person becomes a disciple. When the disciple brings a person to Christ, the disciple-maker takes on the role of a coach and the disciple takes on the role of disciple-maker.
3. The coach assumes that role only after the disciple whom the disciple-maker brought to Christ introduces another person to Jesus as Savior. At this point, a triad has been formed that consists of a disciple, a disciple-maker, and a coach. The new disciple's spiritual growth occurs as he or she participates in a mentoring

relationship with the disciple-maker. The new disciple develops by establishing a relationship with Christ; sharing his or her faith with others, and continuing to be equipped by the disciple-maker and participating in fellowship with other believers.
4. When this new disciple has produced another disciple (fruit), a second triad is established. The disciple becomes a disciple-maker. The new disciple-maker becomes the coach. The relationship between the original coach and disciple-maker continues, creating a cycle with a spiraling effect in the congregation, and the kingdom of God increases within the ministries of the church.

The idea represents many sets of persons in the congregation following this developmental design for Christian maturity. Individuals in the triads overlap since people in the congregation share relationships outside of their inner circles. Also, most people will have more than one circle of friends or ministries they serve.

The first person in this process is the disciple-maker. Disciple-makers seek to pass on to others what they have discovered in their walk of faith. Churches are sustained when growth patterns are established. The second person in the triad is the disciple. Disciples, who are becoming mature Christians, represent the new congregation and will help to sustain the church. They are growing in their relationship with Christ in the context of a supportive community. Each person at this stage is establishing a personal faith relationship with Christ that is foundational, lifelong, and intimate. The third person in this triad is the coach, who assists the new disciple-maker as he or she disciples others. A coach is much like a grandparent. He or she is primarily focused on helping the disciple-maker (the parent) to be successful. The first person to serve as coach is the group facilitator. The coach, the disciple-maker, and the growing disciple form a triad.

Stagnant

Limited spiritual growth causes spiritual stagnation. Spiritual growth produces an urgency to reproduce discipleship in others. A spiritually stagnant church moves around and around in a circle. A church that is growing spiritually experiences spiraling rather than circling. As involvement in activities increases from year to year, the church spirals outside of itself, producing growth.

I have observed some longtime church members remain stagnant with their ministry involvement. In some instances the ministry was vibrant, and in others it was standing still. In a preliminary survey I conducted at one church, I discovered that some Bible teachers did not consider themselves to be disciple-makers. A disciple-maker helps others grow in their relationship with Christ; this is critical to developing a spiritual heritage that produces more disciples. I do not think I will ever fully understand how Sunday-school or Bible-study teachers could fail to see that they are supposed to help others grow. How do we allow people to think that way? Why do we keep them in place without trying to help them strengthen their faith? Someone once said, "The teacher does the most learning," and I believe it. We must provide opportunities for teachers to grow as well. A heavier judgment is on them. "(James 3:1).

The teaching staff should be more involved in Bible study, Sunday school, and other opportunities for studying the Word of God. Persons who teach the Bible should also position themselves to be taught and should pursue relationships that encourage learning. A dark cloud hovers over a congregation that allows persons to stand before classes to teach when they never attend sessions where they are taught. That hinders the church, which should always be trying to cultivate the leadership's vision with the Bible as the central focus for the good of all.

How can a teacher who is never taught hold to the Word of God as truth? (2 Timothy 2:15, 3:16–17, and Titus 1:9). This is an integrity issue. My concern is for the non-Christian as well as the babe in Christ who will not grow because of questions about what others do or fail to do.

Some deacons, deaconesses, and other elected church officials do not attend Bible study or other ministry functions that promote learning the Word of God. Yet they are teachers and deacons who attend church business meetings when a hot topic is on the agenda or they desire to add an issue. This happens in urban and rural churches alike. Still other members seem to be content to show up for weekly worship and to return to their routines with little or no involvement in church ministries.

Evidence of spiritual growth should extend beyond involvement in the same tasks year after year. Many persons are programmatic rather than ministry-minded; for example, people routinely stay on as secretary or treasurer of an auxiliary but do not come to Bible study or sit in any other classes where the Bible is being taught. Many attend programs as opposed to participating in ministry. Ministry involvement offers nurturing support that promotes spiritual growth in others. Teachers involved in Sunday school, children's church, and midweek Bible study should be given opportunities to learn more about the gospel.

I have watched some children grow into clones of their parents; it is sad to see a vibrant child slowly develop a discipleless disposition. It is worse to see that vibrancy squelched by a parent who does not understand the fervor produced by a child's growing relationship with God. It is difficult to watch spiritual malnourishment transform the innocence of children into a discipleship deficit. A lack of involvement in church ministry is often to blame. It is sad that community and school involvement is sometimes higher among people with few links to the church.

One of the saddest situations I have seen in ministry involved a young family that regularly attended Sunday school, Sunday worship services, Wednesday Bible study, and vacation Bible school. At five and seven, and later at eight and twelve, respectively, two of the three children repeatedly could explain the concept of salvation and wanted to be baptized. Their mother would not allow it because she said they were not ready. Whenever one of them would make a mistake, she would say, "You see that. That's how come I know you not ready to be baptized. You not serious 'bout it." I will leave the lifestyle of the mother for another book.

On the other hand, I have observed others who were indifferent for years but became students of the Word. As a result, they became more involved in ministry and showed evidence of fruitfulness in growing relationships with others in the body of believers. They also manifested boldness that did not previously exist in sharing the love of Christ with others. One example is my own spiritual evolution.

Once while observing a Sunday school class, I experienced an "aha moment" concerning the developmental design for Christian maturity. The lesson centered on Peter, and the instructor encouraged students to discover Peter's process of maturing as a Christian. One student said church members must change from their "old ways as a neophyte Christian to an adolescent Christian to a mature Christian." Peter's spiritual evolution offers an example. We see him before he has met Christ, as a disciple, as an ear-cutter, as a disciple-maker after recognizing his error in denying Jesus, and finally as a preacher in 1 and 2 Peter.

Neophytes are babes who believe in Christ but are more easily led by the flesh. Adolescent believers are growing disciples. Mature Christians are growing while they share testimonies and time with others to encourage them to move closer to Christ. Mature Christians are involved in an evolving continuum. Here lies the distinction among church members, disciples, and disciple-makers. I captured the essence of this concept from observations by a student in a Sunday school class. Oh, what power there is in an intimate study and application of God's Word!

You can never know the depth of another person's commitment because public evidence of true discipleship is difficult to assess. However, John 15:8 says that you will know true disciples by their fruit. (John 15:8). This is the key to assessing your status as a disciple. Christians who are disciples share life and pray for one another inside and outside of the church house. How you relate to others demonstrates what you believe; your lifestyle reflects the truth others see. If a person has been living the same way for the last twenty to thirty years, where is the fruit? While we stand on every word of God, we must exercise caution against developing a haughty attitude toward others. Go ahead and acknowledge the fruit you see or don't see in another person; that has ministry implications for church leaders. But place greater emphasis on monitoring what is growing in your own orchard. That is the purpose of *Beyond Discipleship to Relationship*. Your personal spiritual growth matters most.

Disciple-making uses relationship as a catalytic converter; you must have relationships with others in the congregational body. Those relationships must manifest the unconditional love of God. A catalytic converter is a device that uses a catalyst (a medium or a channel) to convert three harmful compounds in car exhaust into harmless compounds. It helps reduce emissions from car engines and fuel systems; it treats exhaust before it leaves the car and removes a lot of pollution.[10] The disciple-maker is also a catalytic converter; he or she does not convert anyone but serves as a channel that changes habits that are harmful to spiritual growth and helps transform lives. Disciple-makers coach disciples through a change process that treats their exhaust (what is coming out) before it pollutes the environment in which they live.

Discipleship is about relationship. When new converts and Christian disciples join a fellowship of believers, they must continue to see the evidence of God's love in the people within that fellowship.

Personal Points to Ponder

What will you do to prevent your spiritual growth from stagnating?

If you observe someone who is spiritually stagnant, what will you do?

Getting Started Personally

Once your church has embraced an approach that values small teams for nurturing members, you should take advantage of the opportunities this arrangement provides. Locate partners who will hold you accountable for who you say you are. Keep in mind that no one person can completely fill that role. In every situation you face, ask God to show you with whom to share. I guarantee that God will place before you exactly the person he has chosen to escort you through that time. You may be celebrating a victory or grieving over a loss of some kind. You may be contemplating a life-altering decision or something not critical at all, just something you want to discuss to gain another Christian perspective. If you ask, God will show you who to include in your intimate circle at that moment.

Getting Started Corporately

Churches that provide opportunities for spiritual growth to people at various stages of Christian development experience increased ministry involvement. Maturing as a Christian requires the opportunity to encounter the Word of God in fellowship with other believers. Churches should not replace existing programs but should find out who is interested in new ones and poll these people for the best time to convene. Churches must meet people where they are in the growth spectrum and offer classes geared toward all stages of Christian development. These classes should then become part of the norm as opposed to programs given special emphasis for a season.

To ensure the effectiveness of this approach, the pastor should inform the congregation about new classes from the pulpit, confirming pastoral support. The success of a course of study hinges on volunteerism rather than on pressure. Churches should also discourage congregants from signing up for a class to "help." They should take a class or participate in a fellowship because they yearn for spiritual growth. The title of a course—"Maturing as a Christian," for example—should be the draw. Adult Christians who have been members of the congregation for an extended period should volunteer. There must be no coercion even when numbers are low. The purpose is not to draw a crowd but to feed the sheep who are ready for a diet with more substance.

During the first session participants should fill out information forms. While organizers are examining the results, a regular sign-up sheet will do to project attendance and to determine the need for space and materials. The church can do a preliminary survey of participants to determine the desire for specific types of training. A follow-up survey can be done to assess the results from the perspective of participants. The second survey should be optional as long as participants are growing and becoming more involved in ministry work.

Barbara A. F. Brehon

Preliminary Survey/"Maturing as a Christian"

Information Sheet

Name
Address   City   State   Zip
Telephone   E-mail

Circle your age group:
12–14   15–18   19–25   26–30   31–35   36–54   55–70   70+

Gender: Male   Female

Check all responses that apply to you.
Do you consider yourself to be a:
Disciple of Christ Jesus (a student of the Word and a follower of his ways)?
Disciple maker (one who helps others to have a growing relationship with Christ)?
Are you a disciple who desires to become a disciple maker?
Are you a disciple maker who desires to train others to be disciple makers?

Do you attend Bible study at this church? Yes No

Which do you attend? How frequently? Which are you teaching?

- ☐ Tuesday/ Noonday
- ☐ Wednesday
- ☐ Thursday/ Midday
- ☐ Sunday school
- ☐ Advanced Bible classes
- ☐ None of the above
- ☐ Other

Please return today to: (Designate someone.)
Thank you.

Reflections before Distributing the Forms

1. Do not be overly concerned about the number of people who show interest or reveal their gender. Feed them.
2. Do not assume that respondents consider themselves to be disciples of Christ. They may be signing up to learn to grow.
3. Do not assume that respondents want to help others gain in faith. Respondents may grow into that role later.
4. Some may desire to help others become disciples or want to train others to become disciple makers. Pray that your judgmental nature allows you to see the authentic fruit they bear.
5. Realize that those who want to help may have to be taught again (Hebrews 5:12).
6. Notice which teachers choose to participate. Some may not choose to participate at all. Why? Is it a question of time? Do they dislike the material? Or do they simply not want to take part? Remember that no one can be forced to participate.
7. Notice which teachers attend sessions they do not teach. This indicates they are willing to feed and to be fed.
8. Do not be surprised if you learn that teachers are eager to participate but do not think of themselves as disciple makers. Perhaps they do not understand the term. Maybe they have been struggling to believe what they have been teaching but now are ready to accept the Lord personally and to grow.
9. Some of those receiving forms may not return them; these people are the tares. Accept that and nurture the wheat.

The survey implies that churches need to provide intentional opportunities for members to experience transformative teaching that produces effective disciples and disciple makers.

Merging Processes

A functional model for maturing Christians emphasizes relationship-building skills. While serving at several churches, I designed an approach for moving beyond discipleship to a more intimate relationship with Christ by extracting components of ministry models proven effective in creating a lifestyle each body of believers could pattern. This strategy provides optimal times for informal sharing during each session. After examining the situation at my church and reviewing preliminary surveys, I chose a curriculum I had previously published, *Maturing as a Christian*.[11]

Having succeeded with this approach at one church, I used a different book, *Moving to the Next Level: Becoming a Fully-Developing Follower of Christ*,[12] at another church. I changed the curriculum to meet different needs, but the process remained the same. *Beyond Discipleship to Relationship* primarily concerns people; material resources must change according to the situation at each church. We must meet people where they are and escort them through a process of perpetual growth.

The process focuses on various aspects of an individual's lifestyle, with the goal of nurturing the person. I assembled ideas gleaned from the literature and from experience. The goal of the process is transformation, using mentors and topics chosen based on the command to make disciples and on the expectation that disciples will be fruitful.

Design

Persons who could become partners in mentoring relationships include members who have been faithful in attending programs and committee meetings and those who have been uninvolved but have sat in the pews. In a mentoring or coaching relationship, one partner has something the other needs. A disciple is enabled by experience to model and to articulate steps to a church member through a developmental process. Church members

Beyond Discipleship to Relationship

who hear from a spiritual coach may eventually respond by witnessing in like manner to persons at home, at work, in organizations and committees, or in the pew. The pew person then learns, shares, and returns to the mentor for encouragement to remain engaged in the disciple-making and spiritual growth process.

A myriad of interrelationships develop and can be reproduced in the congregation. The devoted participant can develop by sharing what he or she learns about Christ with someone else. The new disciple eventually becomes a disciple-maker. The pew person is engaged with the disciple-maker, who is engaged with a coach. The coach, who is a mature Christian, evolves from a disciple/disciple-maker pair. When the disciple effectively shares his or her testimony, a new disciple becomes the third part of a small team. Jesus recruited disciples one or two at a time, then nurtured them.

The disciple sharing the testimony becomes the new disciple-maker; the disciple-maker becomes a coach. These people form a triad that can be multiplied in the congregation. The coach assists the persons he or she has discipled while they disciple others. The coach focuses on strengthening a Christian lifestyle for himself or herself as well as for the disciple-maker, using existing relationships as an anchor. The disciple-maker is not necessarily an officer, Christian education leader, or teacher in the church; he or she could be a person in the pew who is ready and willing and possibly already working toward a deeper spirituality and commitment to Christ.

The key is not to create something new, but to identify a system that will promote continual growth within the congregation. This approach should encourage the imitation of a biblical norm. However, teaching a Bible lesson in church does not necessarily lead to effective discipleship training or disciple-making. After the lesson has been taught, what happens to ensure its application? The ministry design must include opportunities for the learner/disciple to engage the concepts highlighted in the lesson. If people are engaged, they participate and share their experiences. If disciples engage a biblical/spiritual concept, they are more likely to apply it. The application of lessons learned goes beyond knowing what was taught; it extends to daily living and touches the congregation. When disciples take lessons to heart, knowing is equivalent to discipleship. Application is tantamount to disciple-making, a step beyond discipleship.

Teaching the imitation of biblical truths enables the process to advance in the congregation. A developmental approach fosters closer relationships with God among church members. At the first church where I tried this approach, the process included a series of lessons on prayer, stewardship, and witnessing. At the second church, the lessons series addressed relationship with Jesus, responsibility for personal growth, accountability to God and to other believers, and productivity because of increased responsibility and accountability. The lessons a church chooses are not the key; pastoral leadership determines the content of the sessions. The key is teaching Christians ways to grow in relationships with the Lord.

To facilitate this process, I first had to address my relationship with the congregation. I needed to be transparent and explain how God had guided me through levels of spiritual maturity. I acknowledged that my discipleship depended on God and my trust that the Holy Spirit would lead me to him. By observing the changes in me, others could see how God manifests himself. There is no substitute for a testimony. This opened the door to intimacy and trust within the group, providing a solid foundation for the triads that would later form. The disciple must be a disciple-maker and continue to grow, thereby modeling what is expected of Christ's true followers. Leaders who are not disciples are hindrances to church members becoming disciples and to disciples becoming disciple-makers.

The courses were divided into seven sessions. The topics for the two churches were slightly different, mirroring the reading selected to encourage home study.

Topics for the first church were "The Purpose of Prayer," "The Object of Prayer," "A Guide to Effective Prayer," "The Results of Prayer," "God Is the Owner," "Stewardship of Time," "Stewardship of Possessions," "Stewardship of Talents," "Accountable to God," "The Purpose of Witnessing," "Qualifications for Witnessing," "Jesus' Example of Witnessing," and "Power to Witness."

Topics for the second church were "Prayer," "Purity," "Power," "Peace," "Corporate Peace," "Praise," "Participation," "Profession," "Prosperity," "Provision," and "Play."

The goal of each session was to offer participants a chance to share spiritual experiences they had had between sessions. As they voiced their thoughts, they became more resolved to honor their commitment to remain steadfast and were strengthened. Sessions were divided into three themes or units, focusing discussions and honoring the movement of the Holy Spirit during discussions and personal preparation. Persons new to developing a relationship with the Lord need structure to guide them. We helped them to recognize the Holy Spirit as the teacher. (John 14:26 and 1 John 2:27).

When publicizing the classes, it is important to consider that the thematic overview captures the attention of people seeking to develop a closer relationship with Christ. An increase in communication with God improves the disciples' stewardship patterns. Disciples study a more effective prayer life. After identifying areas in their lives that must change to propel Christ to the center, disciples share their testimony with others. Increased prayer and improved stewardship lead disciples to witness to others about the changes God has made in their lives. This produces fruit as family members, coworkers, neighbors, and other church members observe lifestyle changes in these growing Christians, and think, *If God can do that for them, I want some of what they have.* This increases the opportunity for new triads to form.

I anticipated that persons would be more likely to commit to the full course if it had a specific duration. Some of the sessions were held within the same week, others were held a week apart, while others were held two weeks apart. The church and facilitators' calendars were considerations. I believed that outside assignments would offer flexibility and ensure accountability; some had to be monitored more closely than others for the sake of continuity and progress through the process.

The sessions often included impromptu role-playing and discussions with open-ended questions. For example, a participant might want to know what he or she should do or say in a particular situation. Two other participants would be asked to simulate the situation so that this person could see possible Christian responses. In some cases, the participant with the concern would play the role of an opponent to see the other side and to get a better idea of how to react in difficult situations. I rarely used lectures but did not completely avoid them.

The first step in the transformative process addressed individual identity and identity in Christ. Participants had to trust that they were in a safe environment that allowed them to build relationships with mutual confidence. They learned how prayer strengthens the disciple's relationship with God. With this in mind, they could look for what God is doing in every situation in life. Through a series of lessons on prayer, participants heightened their dependence on God and trust in him. A mentor would not assume God's rightful place. Relationships were strengthened in smaller groups outside of the sessions.

Mentoring encouraged growth and helped maintain accountability. Disciples were responsible for initiating an association with someone they respected and trusted. The person chosen as mentor did not have to be a part of the group but had to be a member of the congregation. This requirement supported the goal of increasing disciples' involvement in the congregation. During the sessions, we might briefly discuss the process of seeking a spiritual mentor and maintaining communication with this person. The disciple-maker and the coach would also have to accept responsibility to listen. They would make a verbal commitment regardless of whether they planned on attending our study sessions.

The crucial component of the triads was the testimony of the participants in and outside of the sessions. Their ability to articulate what was happening on the journey confirmed their position in the process. The facilitator (session leader), coach, or disciple-maker then encouraged self-reflection based on Scripture. However, the position of participants on the journey was less important than the fact that they were involved in the process of maturing. The value of mentors was in their willingness to be available, to listen, and to affirm the disciple's identity. Acceptance builds trust. Disciples were taught to expect that from a nurturing relationship or to find another relationship if they thought their spiritual needs weren't being met.

The topic of stewardship followed the unit on prayer because relationship with God and with others is manifested in how we perceive ownership. After spiritual and personal identities are established, our beliefs about God's role in the disciple's life must be addressed. The body is God's temple; it does not belong to us. Possessions are entrusted to us and also belong to God. Finally, we are accountable to God for what we do and how we think. All three of these points affect our relationships. Weak relationships cannot be a proving ground for witnessing for Christ. At the end of the course, participants engaged with each other to witness and to point others to Christ. A more detailed account of each session can be found in appendix A.

As we grow in Christ, we must tell others about him. Experiences with God through Jesus qualify Christians to witness to others. Christ's disciples must live according to his example.

This approach to growing intimate relationships with Christ takes participants a step beyond personal discipleship. It embraces the goal of building relationships with more seasoned disciples as well as with nonbelievers. The testimony of participants validates the positive effect. They accept a lifestyle that includes sharing themselves within the church and the community. Participants take responsibility for seeking nurture as well as providing it to others. They also accept having others hold them accountable for altering undesirable parts of their lifestyles brought to the forefront during their study of God's Word.

Observations from Experiential Encounters

An evaluation session took place three months after the course ended. This session brought together members of a focus group with two of my colleagues. These two persons were in relationship with my church in different ways. They offered differing perspectives to provide balance, which is why they were chosen. Each was beneficial to the process, validating the need for church leaders to embrace shared leadership. Audrey Pryor-Mouizi (A. M.), who is not a member of the congregation, offered unbiased and invaluable reflections. The vivid expressions of V. S., who has been a member of the congregation for eight years, mirrored A. M.'s. V. S. is familiar with the congregation, having played a vital role in the Christian education ministry for four years. Before their involvement in the course, A. H. and V. S. had no connection.

Participants maintained weekly journals that helped to reveal changes and struggles they faced while taking the course. Details of the encounters during the seven sessions plus the summation session can be found in appendix A. What follows is a recapitulation of developmental portraits of five participants five months after the last session.

S. R.

During the summation session, S. R. identified herself as being both a disciple and a disciple-maker who has been maturing as a Christian for seven years. She was baptized as a child and grew up in the same church. She confessed that she might not know the answers to faith-related questions. Her shyness is a hindrance to conversing with strangers, but she sees herself as more of a listener than a speaker. She has many opportunities to provide encouragement by being available to listen others. Since taking the course, S. R. has continued her involvement with ushering, Sunday school, and Bible study; she is concerned about overburdening herself. She has suffered with physical maladies brought on by extreme stress.

C. H.

She affirmed that her life has changed since taking the class. C. H. has shed her guarded personality and is now more willing to share her faith. Previously she would not testify, whereas now she acknowledges God. In addition, she has begun to accept responsibility to initiate conversation that builds rapport needed to grow relationships with other Christians. C. H. said she felt safe about expressing her gut feelings to her disciple-maker. While listening to others in similar relationships in the focus group, she was able to synthesize her position in a personal manner. She now uses journaling to reflect and to relieve stress. C. H. said that her best friend, who is unchurched, could see that she has changed and attended church with her.

C. H. said she needed a smaller group than Sunday school provided and would not previously attend Bible study. She said that learning about God was fulfilling but lonely. She occupies herself with many things, including work, home, and church once a week. C. H. is involved in Sunday school, Bible study, and worship services. She attends more services and other church events than she did before being involved with "Maturing as a Christian." She is taking piano lessons at our church and expressed an interest in the drama ministry. C. H. was uncertain about what God wanted her to be but now has more clarity. She has enrolled in Norfolk State University with a major in journalism.

D. C.

She could not see that she had grown; however, D. C. now tells her family that she will not stop going to church. She had not previously exhibited such boldness. D. C. cited the fact that she runs to prayer and praise before Wednesday Bible study, which she had not previously done. She said that her motive was more than prayer and praise; the testimonies are a help to her. She has given a brief testimony on occasion. D. C. also continues her involvement with the usher board. Others commented about her smile, implying that her greeting at the doors of the church is not a small thing. D. C. has admitted to experiencing bouts of depression, and she found the affirmation extremely empowering.

C. O.

C. O. is a baby Christian who decided to take the course "Maturing as a Christian" because he was concerned about praying more effectively. Now he prays several times a day and professes a desire to be a follower. C. O. confessed that he was not growing, yet has testimony of some change. For example, we watched a Bible-based movie at a fellowship with the group and he pointed out something that was not in the Bible. He said he could not have done that a year ago. Moreover, he said he attends a lot more Bible study classes and has come a long way. He affirmed his position as a disciple but is not yet a disciple-maker. He envisions going to Africa to teach people about God. After taking the study course, C. O. acknowledged a need to do something for somebody else; he wants to work with children and do mission work. C. O. said he wants to do more than take pictures for the public relations committee, with which he was involved when the course began.

A. D.

Journaling has facilitated growth in A. D. She can bridle her tongue with family members and records disappointments and frustrations. She is now open to change and commented that God's purpose has priority over her own, though putting him first is a struggle. Because of her experiences with God, she is less likely to question why some situations exist. The classes confirmed that she should seek to learn God's will rather than ask for things that she wanted. She tearfully expressed her gratitude for the sessions; A. D. professed to have acquired much from the guidance provided. She is determined to refer to the Bible to make sense out of what is going on in her life, looking for God's purpose in her circumstances. She finds comfort and assurance in God in contrast with her previous uncertainty.

After going only sporadically, A. D. is now committed to attending Sunday school every week, taking her grandson. A. D. had not considered herself a disciple-maker until others enlightened her after hearing her testimony. Upon reflection, she recalled a friend who now seeks Scripture guidance from her during long-distance calls; her grandson and others also turn to her for spiritual help. A. D. will continue to sing in the gospel choir and now wants to become involved in the women's ministry, specifically helping women who have fought drug addiction and are now leaving prison. She is making herself more available to do ministry in the church.

Summary of the Encounters

The participants want to go to another spiritual level. During the summation session, they showed an increased desire to work in the church or the community. They clearly prefer a smaller setting for learning to apply the Bible; they want something more personal than what larger groups offer. The course promoted Christian maturity and merged participants into church ministries. The church does not give people the chance to talk in small groups as part of a routine study process. We do a lot of teaching, but we should offer more opportunities for intimate engagement.

The approach for building relationships used in the triads became an empowering tool. Empowerment was not an expected outcome, but became evident in testimonies by participants. They became aware of dormant gifts and desires. Matriculation through "Maturing as a Christian" helped them not only to recognize those gifts and desires but to explore and deploy them.

The success of the developmental approach for growing intimate relationships with the Lord was anchored on the perspective of participants.

A preliminary survey identified participants, who completed a seven-session series to establish triads for spiritual mentoring. A follow-up survey was done to determine the effectiveness of the course based on participants' perceptions of themselves.

We targeted church members who were interested in Christian growth, expecting to create a desire by participants to become more involved in church ministries. The church should provide opportunities for people to mature spiritually. One way to do that is to use triads that function informally outside of a classroom setting, developing strategies that propel spiritual growth in an emotionally safe environment.

The training was designed to create a place where participants would confide issues of personal growth. In addition, the training proposed effective Christian approaches to move disciples to help others strengthen their relationships with God. The training was designed to establish a process allowing church members to cultivate relationships within the congregation, nurturing the development of other members. While studying the lessons, disciples would not only learn for personal growth but would share with others the changes that developed from the lessons. The disciple-makers listening to the disciples would encourage these students, who were now motivated to share with more people, creating a ripple effect throughout the congregation.

Listening to the testimonies of participants during the evaluation session affirmed a need for the church to encourage the development of small groups that create an atmosphere for intimate sharing and for growth. The course of study was not the key to the growth of participants; the ability to safely reveal themselves and to discuss issues openly with a few trusted others was a greater aid to Christian maturity. Many people do not have that opportunity at home, and the church must consistently offer lovingly protected places of nurture. It is sad to think that people cannot find a safe place to deal with their growing pains in the church house. We must change that by living with integrity and holding personal confidences as sacred communication not to be tattled, gossiped about, or shared at the dinner table.

The topics were selected with the aim of equipping disciples to nurture spiritual disciplines without feeling threatened. The topics were supposed to provide a platform to help participants begin a lifelong process of spiritual development. The initial proposal was to motivate participants who identified themselves as disciples toward growth. The course was intended to encourage participants to build relationships that foster ongoing nurture and to be accountable for those relationships. The topics served the purpose of mentally relocating disciples and were extremely successful.

Collegial Support

Below are excerpts from an electronic mail message received from Audrey Pryor-Mouizi, who facilitated the evaluation session with participants three months after the last study session ended at the first church.

> Just wanted to let you know that last night's session was intriguing … When I woke up this morning I thought about how God operates. You initially set out to develop a process/plan whereby Christians would become disciple-makers. As I listened to the group last evening … it dawned on me that some had become disciple-makers (the lady who is teaching now … she specifically said she talks to people about the Lord)—some were engaging in disciple-making and didn't know it (the grand mom), some others had an increased desire to become a disciple-maker, and at least one wasn't there yet … if my memory serves me correctly.
>
> I thought about how it was that I thought the process would be linear … that people would emerge from it with a 'voila' moment—and suddenly be disciple-makers. But what I observed is an evolution … still in process … then I thought about how it is that our God is not a linear God. God is a God who gets us where we need to go … it's a process.
>
> On another note, early this morning as I lay awake thinking about your work, the Lord let me see that it has wider implications than we can imagine … And, as we know, Jesus called us to go get and care about them.

The notion came to me that your work broadens our horizons … it pushes us toward where it is God meant for us to be—disciple-makers. I thought about how awesome it would be if the work of disciple-making became an integral part of every new member's class. The point made and taught that we are not only called into relationship with the Lord Jesus, but we're called to help others get there, too … that's another whole way of doing church!

As I listened to the group last evening, it gave me an opportunity to see how we make excuses for not helping others come into relationship with the Lord Jesus Christ. We make all kinds of excuses! But we don't fail to tell our friends, families, and strangers about a sale that's going on, or a free giveaway of some sort! (I'm not being hard on the group … I see and hear the same thing at my church … and churches all over. People have all kinds of excuses for not disciple making!)

PART 4

**Reckoning
Conclusion**

"Sunset"
Virginia Beach, Virginia, March 2012

Reckoning

The goal of this process of building relationship with Christ is not success measured by a contrived standard, but consistency that leads the disciple, the disciple-maker, and the coach to closer connections with God. Success can be measured only by the testimony of participants. A final reckoning depends on determining whether the premises of *Beyond Discipleship to Relationship* are sound.

Hoping to do more effective work with a small group, I had to remain practical to be sensitive to participants' needs. I had to be more people-minded and compassionate; I used journaling to record thoughts in the first few days after each session. This helped me to focus on participants and to keep their growth my main goal. Sharing my journaling set an example for their journaling. As I facilitated the Christian growth process, I grew in God's grace as did participants. A teacher indeed does the most learning. The lessons on stewardship convicted me of poor time management. Years later I still wrestle with effectively and obediently using my time.

During the sixth session, the group became less involved in discussion. This was the first session in which participants were held accountable for leading others into a conversation about their relationship with God. People becoming comfortable with personal growth were being asked to involve themselves in someone else's growth, and that was not easy for some. The theological foundation of John 15:8 became acutely apparent during this session. If people were establishing firmer relationships with God and with others through Jesus Christ, they were accountable for producing fruit. Disciple-making is a step beyond discipleship.

I found increased involvement in congregational ministries. Initially all but one participant was involved in at least one ministry. Three persons reported new involvement while five indicated an increased commitment to current ministry involvement. The post-assessment showed that one person had decided to become involved but was still not participating in any ministry. Within a few months of the last session, this person had agreed to serve on the finance committee, had enrolled in piano classes, and had discussed joining the drama ministry, all at the church.

A discussion in the follow-up session revealed displeasure with Sunday school classes participants were attending and with a specific ministry. Perhaps their gifts were not needed in these situations; the growing disciples could explore other church activities. Rather than giving participants a platform to complain, I asked questions to goad them to explore ministries that aligned with their interests and spiritual gifts.

Pastoral leaders should require teachers to spend a specified amount of time in corporate study of the Bible and hold them accountable. Teachers might be requested to attend Bible study at least once a month on Tuesday, Wednesday, Thursday, or Sunday evening. How can leaders expect others to commit to their meetings and other activities when they do not observe Timothy's lesson to present yourself as an approved workman? *(*2 Timothy 2:15).

Participants shared disciple-making experiences. Prior to the sessions, one participant acknowledged a desire to become a disciple-maker. Afterward, he recounted telling a lady at a Laundromat that everything belongs to God. The testimonies of participants validated the need for the conscious pursuit of goals. One participant wrote about being able to put lessons into daily practice. Another reported difficulty in handling family matters for eighteen years. This participant was initially the most reluctant to share, but began to reveal herself midway through the sessions and made a commitment to more faithful attendance at Bible study. Another student expressed appreciation for reaching an unexpected spiritual level. She attributed this to the way her classmates received her, and she gave credit to God for the opportunity. After the sessions ended, three more participants stated a desire to become disciple-makers.

The church will experience a phenomenal increase in involvement when it provides opportunities for intimate sharing that target developing disciple-makers. A congregation will always have those who do not participate in Bible classes or ministry; the tares will crop up among the wheat. However, the intimacy of the smaller group combined with Bible classes facilitates spiritual growth for those who want it. This is where the church will find its future.

All participants wanted to see the sessions expanded by several weeks. During a discussion in the last session, participants recommended that a study of spiritual gifts follow the current curriculum. One participant suggested more journal sharing, and another wanted more teaching. Still another participant suggested that the church provide regular follow-up sessions on a long-term basis. This respondent was absent from the follow-up session and later invited everyone to dinner after the worship service on the second Sunday in December.

Based on the evaluation, I initially thought that the material we used should be expanded. However, after a few years of consideration, I believe that the brevity of the sessions propelled participants to seek the fellowship of church ministries. These sessions should remain short-term with a definite end after five to seven weeks. This will discourage participants from becoming dependent on the group and turning it into a church clique. Rather, they will become dependent on the Lord in healthy spiritual relationships with others as part of the ministry.

Strengths

At my church, the disciple and disciple-maker pairs have proven to be most effective outside of the classroom. Intimacy was developing as early as the first session. Participants expressed concerns regarding biblical interpretations, personal and spiritual growth, and revelations about God, themselves, and significant others. They affirmed and encouraged one another. Midway through the sessions, testimonies showed that the process was working; participants were growing.

Before being required to identify a disciple-maker for the sessions, A. D. had chosen one. This is natural for Christians who decide to strengthen their relationship with God through Jesus Christ. She was ready to grow, and the course nudged her forward. The lesson is that persons who identify themselves as Christ's disciples will participate in courses designed to nurture spiritual-growth relationships. A course like this should be a regular part of a church's teaching ministry.

The group dynamics changed after a visit to the Whistle Stop Ice Cream Shop. The fellowship that began at the ice cream parlor has continued.

Several soirees have been held since the conclusion of the sessions with plans to do monthly or at least bimonthly gatherings organized and facilitated by participants. The relationships of pairs that formed have continued to strengthen, but participants are not cliquish or exclusive. C. M. and C. O. maintain camaraderie. D. C. has expressed concern for C. H. because they share similar circumstances. S. R. has included her sixteen-year-old son in the fellowship gatherings; C. M. has included not only his mother but another male from the congregation.

C. H. has decided to become a part of the drama ministry; she says she likes to act. Previously, she was guarded and reserved; now she is free to be herself. A. H.'s brother submitted his life to Christ and became a candidate for baptism five months after the sessions concluded. She told me that she thought of me when he made the decision. (I never had any contact with him.)

Weaknesses

Participants were extremely communicative though excessively dependent on the facilitator. I considered more follow-ups between sessions. Later I recognized that this would have heightened participants' dependence on me. I volunteered to be the disciple-maker for D. C. because of her anxiety at the thought of revealing herself to someone. Growing emotional, she said, "It's so much stuff. It's personal." Two others asked me to be their disciple-maker, but doing this would have made it difficult to objectively observe the process. Rather than accept, I encouraged them to collaborate with each other throughout the sessions. That worked.

A weakness in my guidance of the sessions became clear when S. R. said, "We have a good relationship together." I could have probed into her perspective on what makes a relationship "good." She had identified herself as a disciple- maker before the course, and I missed an opportunity to explore possibilities for growth with affirming relationships. Doing this might have enlightened the others. However, A. M. addressed portions of this point during the evaluation session. In addition, I did not follow up with S. R. about her negative and hindering friend. I found it difficult to do an assessment while coaching spiritual growth and Christian nurture.

Shared leadership would lessen the dependence of participants on the facilitator/coach.

Individuals readily attended sessions on nurturing the faith of others. The church has a rich history of providing learning opportunities on a variety of topics. If we teach about a subject, members will consider it important and pursue it. In fact, during session five, C. O. admitted his awkwardness about approaching someone to become an accountability partner, or spiritual mentor. He confessed that he did not know what to say. The course had created the environment for him to comfortably share, and he was immediately nurtured for growth in that area. The majority of the responses came from fellow participants.

Recommendations

Courses specifically targeting Christian nurture should become a permanent part of the teaching ministry. At least once annually, a short-term course should be available to help persons assist others in strengthening their relationship with God. The course might be titled "How to Disciple Others." As participants become more aware of strategies that employ disciple-making elements, the idea of coaching would be affirmed without altering the custom of teaching within the church. Coaching would be a natural byproduct of the sessions, though it would not be identified by that term. Terminology isn't nearly as important as providing the opportunity for spiritual growth. Midway through the developmental course, disciples were evolving into disciple-makers and disciple-makers were becoming coaches, though we never used those words.

Suggestions

- Require teachers to be Bible students in corporate settings within the church so they practice what they teach.
- Include short-term courses of study designed to nurture spiritual-growth relationships in an intimate environment. To accommodate personal particularities, smaller groups would meet before the subsequent session to reflect on the lessons taught.

- Include a short-term course of study designed to nurture disciple-makers, and make them a routine topic in the teaching ministry of the church.
- Address the need for intimacy within ministries for easier assimilation of growing disciples at all levels of spiritual maturity.

Conclusion

Other churches should have little trouble applying this approach. The one circumstance that might be an obstacle is the use of small groups within an existing ministry model. However, if the congregation is accustomed to management committed to shared leadership, the empowerment of the triad will be better understood. No other circumstances would prohibit replicating it within congregations of differing size or geographic region.

Congregations concerned about their well-being should note that youths who see adults engaged in a spiritual growth process are more likely to grow through a similar process toward Christian maturity. The young are the disciple-makers of the future church; therefore adult church members are the link to a new generation of disciples. The contemporary church must develop a spiritual heritage that will last. New disciples who are becoming mature disciples are the new generation, which is ageless.

Be at peace, positioned for intimacy with the Lord. Seek divine direction each minute of every day. Move beyond discipleship to deeper relationship with the Lord, sitting with him regularly, learning and practicing his ways. Yes, Jesus is the soothing balm that heals all wounds whether they be physical, emotional, or spiritual.

There Is a Balm in Gilead

Traditional African American Spiritual

Sometimes I feel discouraged and think my work's in vain,
But then the Holy Spirit revives my soul again.
There is a balm in Gilead to make the wounded whole;
There is a balm in Gilead to heal the sin-sick soul.
If you cannot preach like Peter, if you cannot preach like Paul,
You can tell the love of Jesus and say, "He died for all."
There is a balm in Gilead to make the wounded whole;
There is a balm in Gilead to heal the sin-sick soul.
If you can't pray like Peter, if you can't pray like Paul,
Go home and tell your neighbor, "He died to save us all."
There is a balm in Gilead to make the wounded whole;
There is a balm in Gilead to heal the sin-sick soul.
Don't ever feel discouraged, for Jesus is your friend;
And if you lack for knowledge, he'll never refuse to lend.
There is a balm in Gilead to make the wounded whole;
There is a balm in Gilead to heal the sin-sick soul.

Background of the Lyrics

The Israelites were blind to God's will, and he allowed the Babylonian captivity following the people's great sins in the valley of slaughter. The prophet Jeremiah mourned for the slain and for the Israelites' position with their God. Weeping for the people of Israel, who were fallen in shame, he asked if there was a balm in Gilead. (Jeremiah 8:22). He felt despair after King Nebuchadnezzar's two-year siege of Jerusalem. The Old Testament prophet asked a question, and the songwriter says that Jesus is the balm.

Each Christian is the balm God has sent into the world. We must show compassion for others. We must dress the wounds of the people so that they experience the love of the Lord. By meeting people where they sit, we fulfill the Great Commission to go and make disciples. (Matthew 28:19). Mature Christians can escort others into a perpetually growing relationship with the Lord of love. The fruit you bear shows your discipleship. (John 15:8).

John 17: Jesus' Prayer

My favorite prayer in the Bible is Jesus' prayer found in John 17. It speaks to the past, the present, and the future. The Lord prays for himself, for his disciples, for me, and for the world. I feel great joy that Jesus prayed for me so very long ago. How could I not want to be more intimate with him?

Appendix A

The Seven Session Components

1. Exploring the topic "The Purpose of Prayer," session one uncovered a distinction between desires of the flesh and spiritual desires. Matthew 26:41 was discussed. Praying for something that gratifies the flesh is different from acknowledging the supremacy of God's will. The session gave attention to prayers that could help participants avoid conversations with God that yield to fleshly temptations. A Christian communicates with God through Jesus Christ to remain reconciled to God. A believer must exercise caution in prayer to recall its purpose. A person's desire should not be the object of prayer. To re-center on the Lord, participants were directed to 1 Chronicles 29:11.
2. Session two coupled the topics "The Object of Prayer" and "A Guide to Effective Prayer." Participants were expected to write a three-sentence prayer exalting God. Isaiah 59:1 helped them to grasp the point that iniquities separate us from God. Prayer is not effective when sin goes unconfessed. Participants were encouraged to use the triads outside of class to further wrestle with thoughts and feelings emerging during the sessions. We made it clear that each person's privacy must be respected and that no one should feel forced to disclose personal details. The development of an effective triad would allow a person to do that without coercion.
3. Session three hinged on performance of assignments calling for application of the topics discussed. Participants were expected to delve into Scripture rather than depend on statements made by the facilitator. "The Results of Prayer" and "God Is the Owner" were topics for the third session. The process of maturing is advanced when participants experience success. They were asked

to share what happens when they pray and to describe under what circumstances God responded to their prayers. Again, we made it clear that privacy must be respected and that no one should feel forced to disclose personal details. Participants were to focus on the process; Jesus knows the private details. During the week leading to this session, participants reflected on Philippians 4:13. Their ability to articulate empowered them to proceed through the process. We presented few lectures so that they would be better able to hear from God on their own.

Transition into stewardship further facilitated creation of a lifestyle that cultivates relationships with Christ. Given the amount of time needed to discuss prayer and upcoming topics, participants were encouraged to pursue church ministries that addressed those areas. Nurturing can continue for the disciple within other church groups when the triad effectively functions. The study group was not to be permanent but cyclical within the teaching ministry of the church. Adherence to the process would increase involvement in other ministries.

Participants were given an opportunity to discuss their interpretations of 1 Corinthians 6:19. We had two purposes in mind. First, they would practice articulating their thoughts. Second, they would learn to rely on personal Bible reading and reflection. With trust established, participants would have an environment conducive to asking questions about Bible reading skills and the facilitator could suggest developing skills that were obviously lacking. Many people cannot do this in larger groups, even if the facilitator is dynamic and well liked. Flaws are generally cloaked in larger settings and often go unaddressed. Moreover, participants were beginning to accept responsibility for their spiritual growth through active involvement. We wanted to encourage sharing in smaller groups, which provided more intimacy and more trust.

4. The fourth session combined three topics: "Stewardship of Time," "Stewardship of Possessions," and "Stewardship of Talents." The assignment for this session was to identify specific things participants could do to become better stewards. The Bible lessons

included Mark 13:33, Matthew 23:23, and Romans 12:3. We combined several passages to help participants become better time managers and make sure to include God daily. If they could do that for this study, they would likely continue doing it after completing the course. If you develop the discipline to do something for twenty-one days or more, it becomes a habit. What better habit to develop than moving beyond discipleship to relationship with God?

To promote the idea of process, participants discussed stages of life. They were asked to create a personal timeline from birth to death, then identify where they saw themselves on that continuum. Based on what they perceived, they would be in position to define or redefine what to do next. Giving is a valuable concept. Realizing that God owns everything, including their bodies and their possessions, Christ's disciples seek to please him. Their giving should not grieve the One they profess to follow. Stewardship is part of a process that must be developed and nurtured. Stewardship complements discipleship.

Participants were asked to meditate on two questions: How does a disciple surrender possessions and abilities to God? What will you do differently to show that you believe the verses of Scripture being studied? There were no expected responses, but participants had to process information through the filter of their lifestyles. Every session focused on relationship with God and communicating spiritual growth in safe relationships. It was important for participants to articulate their responses rather than remain silent listeners.

5. Session five moved the group toward more accountability. Whether we are wasteful and dishonest or frugal and have integrity, we are responsible to God for what we do and what we neglect. Participants pondered points from Luke 16:1 as they shared what they would have said or done if they were the rich employer asking for an account from an employee. And if they were the stewards in this lesson, how would they have responded to their employer? We used John 15:8 to show that disciples are expected to bear fruit. When we recognize that we are accountable to God for

being productive, we recognize the need for witnessing. Maturing Christians must tell others about their relationship with Christ. Accepting discipleship means sharing for the sake of Christ. With that in mind, the study session transitioned to Acts 22:15 and John 4:39.

6. The passage from Acts helped participants to delineate simple "Qualifications for Witnessing" during session six. Philip was committed to following the Lord and to sharing his faith. He obeyed the Lord's voice because he had heard it before. He could distinguish the voice of the Lord from the voice of the enemy. The first qualification for witnessing is to make certain that we have an experience of Christ to retell. We must commit our intellects, our emotions, and our wills to God. Second, we must make sure that we have no unconfessed sin in our lives. We must be filled with the Holy Spirit. He is the One who gives power to witness. Third, we must be prepared to communicate our faith with others.

    The study from the gospel of John illustrated "Jesus' Example of Witnessing." Participants were asked to share how they first received the good news of Christ, then compare what each of these testimonies had in common. Participants were then asked to identify the steps that Jesus took in witnessing to the Samaritan woman and compare them with the testimonies of the group. Participants explored the topic "Example of Witnessing," suggesting commonplace experiences or natural opportunities that could be used to open a conversation that leads someone to Christ.

7. Once participants had looked at opportunities to advance in Christian maturity, the group examined the "Power to Witness." Session seven focused on Acts 1:8 and 4:31, verses that concern witness empowerment. Jesus promised that his followers would receive power when the Holy Spirit came upon them. When the Holy Spirit descended upon the disciples in the upper room, they were empowered to speak the Word of God with boldness. The Holy Spirit makes the Word of God irresistible; we need only share our experiences with others.

Appendix B

"Maturing as a Christian" Course Review

Write a brief summary of what you gleaned from each session.

Session #	Day	Date	Time	Topic
1	Monday	May 17, 2004	6:30–8:00 p.m.	The Purpose of Prayer
2	Monday	May 24, 2004	6:30–8:00 p.m.	The Object of Prayer / A Guide to Effective Prayer
3	Monday	June 7, 2004	6:30–8:00 p.m.	The Results of Prayer / God Is the Owner
4	Tuesday	June 15, 2004	6:30–8:00 p.m.	Stewardship of Time Stewardship of Possessions Stewardship of Talents
5	Monday	July 5, 2004	6:30–8:00 p.m.	Accountable to God / The Purpose of Witnessing
6	Thursday	July 8, 2004	6:30–8:00 p.m.	Qualifications for Witnessing / Jesus' Example of Witnessing
7.	Monday	July 26, 2004	6:30–8:00 p.m.	Power to Witness

Appendix C

"Maturing as a Christian" Evaluation Form

Name (Optional):   Date:

Directions: Answer the questions using a scale from 1 to 5. Write the number in front of each item.

1=Not at all   3=Somewhat   5=Exceeded expectations

Did this course helped you to mature as a Christian?
Did this course help you to decide to use more of your God-given gifts?
Was the material presented in a manner that you could easily understand?
Did the facilitator seem to have knowledge of the material presented?
Did you like the class structure (assignments, group discussions, facilitation)?
Was the book helpful to you?
Would you recommend this book or this course to a friend?
Did this course challenge you to change any aspect of your life?
Do you feel you have arrived at or are on your way to another level of spiritual maturity?

1. How long have you held church membership?
2. Since this course began, have you become involved in a church ministry?
   Yes No   If yes, what ministry?
3. If you were already involved in a ministry, did this course cause you to be more fully committed to it? Yes Somewhat No
4. If you are not involved in a church ministry, do you plan to become involved in the near future? Yes Possibly No

5. What suggestions would you make to improve the course?
   ☐ Longer class time ☐ Add more weeks to the program
   ☐ More journal sharing ☐ More teaching ☐ More group discussion ☐ Less group discussion ☐ Less teaching
   ☐ Other

You may give your final thoughts below.

Appendix D

Experiential Encounters Journal

The focus group participated in sessions under the umbrella of a course entitled "Maturing as a Christian." The course title and the title of the study book were the same. The schedule for the sessions was published in the weekly newsletter and included time, place, and topics. (See appendix B.) The pastor spoke just once from the pulpit to ensure that participants were self-motivated. The following account is based on field experience with the disciple-making ministry approach. I maintained a weekly journal; a verbatim account was compiled shortly after each session. Seven sessions were planned; an eighth session was not a part of the original strategy. This session resulted from a lack of closure in session seven and proved invaluable to the process. The summation session brought together the members of the focus group with two of my colleagues to facilitate.

Session 1

The first session was entitled "The Purpose of Prayer." Along with the pastor, four participants were present: A. D., C. H., S. R., and W. S. The session commenced with the completion of an information sheet. Introductions followed, and participants offered information about themselves. They were told to reveal only what they wanted to make known. A fifty-seven-year-old female said she had been in church all of her life and realized when she was fifty-four that she did not know Jesus for herself. She said this course was an answer to her prayers.

I offered an overview of the course, explaining the concept. I told participants that they always had a choice about whether to share and said that confidentiality was a mandate, with the understanding that I might share information with the pastor. However, any participant not wishing to have him informed could trust in confidentiality. The facilitator was placed in a position to model the process being used: the pastor was the coach or accountability partner to the disciple-maker/facilitator. As the process began, the terminology we used had to be adjusted so that participants could understand. I have incorporated expressions they used to describe encounters with the process.

I introduced the curriculum and explained procedures; participants were expected to read and to complete assignments outside of class so that class time would go toward discussion and would focus on facilitating the process. I explained the terms *triad, coach, disciple-maker,* and *disciple*. Next we discussed the topic, using Scripture and the outline of the book *Maturing as a Christian.*[13]

The first assignment was to pray to find the right coach or accountability partner. It did not have to be a person present but someone who could be a confidant willing to work with the facilitator. Participants were also asked to choose a member of the congregation. The goal was to learn ways to channel energy into opportunities to glorify God with a partner. The second assignment was to write a three-sentence prayer exalting God. Participants were encouraged to read that prayer when circumstances appeared to be dismal and they wanted to overcome depression and dismay.

Session 2

The second session was held one week after the first. Of those enrolled, three had completed the preliminary survey. Seventy-five percent of those pre-registered were present, and 68 percent of those who returned completed the assignment outside of class, choosing a person to mentor them (a disciple-maker, who would hold them accountable while nurturing them). Those present were A. D., C. H., J. S., D. C., C. M., and W. S. Participants were encouraged to contact S. R., who was absent. She was working unexpected hours.

Two new persons were the first to arrive, and I gave them an overview of the course and reviewed the first session. Then we had a question-and-answer period regarding the purpose and the structure of the course. I reiterated that participants were involved in a process designed to free them from stagnation and to make them growing Christians who could help others strengthen relationships with God through Jesus Christ. I explained that an assessment at the end of the seven sessions would be accomplished through their testimony. Pairs were established and included the newcomers. The facilitator served as the coach, thus forming several triads simultaneously. New group members were encouraged to prayerfully consider partnerships and would be given the opportunity to select another disciple-maker/mentor.

The topics for the second week were "The Object of Prayer" and "A Guide to Effective Prayer." The discussion among three of the five participants was intense and emotional at times; all three were female. No one dominated the sharing. Twice someone mentioned needing spiritual growth in a specific situation, and another participant assisted with testimony about a similar circumstance.

Participants noted that interruptions occur when spending quiet time with God. A. D. said she was not where she once was with God, and she told her husband that she needed to spend time with the Lord. She would prepare him before she started. She would open her Bible, place her journal nearby, and wait for a minute or so. Eventually her husband left her alone because he saw that this time was sacred for her.

W. S. mentioned meeting a lady the previous Saturday who said she got depressed when she walked into the church. We are supposed to carry the Word of God inside of us, and we should enter his house prepared to worship and praise him. W. S. said he could relate to her because he, too, had felt that way. Someone asked, "How does one move from being depressed to praise and worship?" This movement is a process that must be nurtured. The facilitator was present when the discussion occurred, and sensed the lady's plea for assistance to overcome her depression. Her change in posture appeared to position her to receive all that was said afterward so that she could absorb what she needed. A. D. expressed appreciation for this discussion and said it helped her deal with her situation. She added that she needed to look for God and not be so focused on what was wrong. Within a few days, the facilitator invited the lady to our sessions. She politely said she would consider attending, but she never did.

W. S., who is a deacon, asked that we spend more time discussing effective prayer and communication with God. The group's initial response was to pray about it; in the following session, we encouraged his participation in the prayer ministry. A coach must be aware of opportunities to plant seeds in people that will not only nurture them but will encourage them to join church ministries. The purpose of the sessions was to prompt participants to be more involved in ministries rather than to become dependent on the gatherings. We redirected the discussion, using the table of contents in the book *Maturing as a Christian* to review and urge completion of the readings outside of class. We again urged that participants use the triads to complement their daily walk with God.

Three assignments were expected before the next session. First, participants were to be intentional about praying more frequently, bearing in mind that the Holy Spirit was their prayer partner. In addition, they were to seek out the disciple-maker/accountability partner to discuss what they had experienced. The second assignment was to specify what they could do to be better stewards that week. I reminded them that they would have an opportunity for sharing. Since communicating with God through prayer is more than giving, telling, confessing, and praising, the third assignment was to work on ways of listening to God.

Session 3

All of those registered were present: A. D., C. H., C. M., S. R., D. C., and C. O. In addition, all of the participants had completed the assignment outside of class. The pastor did a walk-through near the beginning of the session; at that time, only one person was present. C. O. was new to the group, but we did not go over the information covered in the first two sessions. When the others arrived, he was more comfortable with the content and with the group dynamics.

Two topics were covered in the third session; the first was "The Results of Prayer." Since this course encourages participants to become active in ministries, I told the group to contact a member of the prayer ministry for additional development in that area. Just as I said that the prayer ministry was available to assist the congregation with prayer needs, three persons from that ministry walked past the room. I invited them to share with us for a moment.

The core ministry leader, a team leader, and a member of the team provided an overview of what the prayer ministry offers. The core ministry leader said that one can take anything to God through prayer, including desires, emotions, and fears. God is always on duty. The team leader mentioned the monthly meetings, the prayer box, and the prayer written weekly for the church newsletter, all providing opportunities for prayer experiences. Anyone could write a prayer and place it in one of two prayer boxes, and a team member would retrieve it, read it, and lift that concern before the Lord more than once each week.

The team member said that the group members prayed for one another as well as for outreach. Each month members shared with residents at an assisted living facility neighboring the church. In addition, prayer vigils were held to lift military families, the nation, and families in general. Prayer walks were held for the annual church and youth revivals. The time concluded with class participants being given an opportunity to ask questions. This was the perfect way to end the first of three sections of our study. In the future, we will invite persons from the prayer ministry to be involved during the concluding session on prayer. Following prayer, we will discuss stewardship and witnessing.

This session was more spiritually intense than previous sessions. During the second half of the lesson, "God Is the Owner," participants were asked to recognize three truths: 1) God has possession of our bodies, 2) Christians embody the Holy Spirit upon a profession of faith in Jesus Christ, and 3) the body is a temple (1 Corinthians 6:19). Therefore Christians are stewards of something that belongs to God. He entrusts us to take care of the body because it is his and because the Holy Spirit dwells there. Consequently, Christians must guard the entrances to the sanctuary; every opening of the body is a place through which appropriate or inappropriate things can enter. Christians must not defile the space the Holy Spirit is supposed to occupy. They must exercise caution about what they see, smell, ingest, hear, or otherwise allow into their bodies. God's presence is at stake. The Spirit of God and the spirit of the enemy will not occupy the same space at the same time; one will leave.

This thought penetrated the consciousness of listeners. All were silent; then responses varied. S. R. walked to another area of the room and sat on the floor. Her face turned red as she communicated with God. A. D. grabbed her face as tears saturated it. She, too, moved to another area of the room and communicated with God. Class continued and we discussed how God can teach us to be better managers of his blessings. Learning hinges on our communication with him. Effective communication with God involves petition or praise but also receiving instruction or correction.

Session 4

The fourth session dealt with "Stewardship of Time," "Stewardship of Possessions," and "Stewardship of Talents." A. D., C. H., C. M., D. C., and C. O. attended. The plan was to use the course study book for this session. As we began the discussion at lesson six, the topic of journaling arose. (Psalm 62:8). C. H. said she was in a different place with journaling. She used it to reflect and to relieve. A. D. had started journaling as well; she did this to prevent bad thoughts from coming out of her mouth. Her accountability partner encouraged her to record disappointments and frustrations.

C. H. had called the pastor to discuss her situation. She had told him that the last session explained the Holy Spirit and that attending the session and reading lesson six had helped her. A few days after the second session, the pastor had told me that someone had mentioned the class to him. He had said that this person was being helped a great deal.

C. O. said that his son had died and that coming to church helped; he recognized that he (C. O.) was in the right place. A. D. said that she had been in her previous church for ten years but did not learn or grow. At our church she no longer felt spiritually bankrupt. She felt that she was under construction and in constant communication with God. C. H. said that her best friend had seen a difference in her. She asked to change her accountability partner because W. S. had not made himself available. He had contacted her in the church aisle a couple of times and asked how she was doing, but she said that was not enough.

In an earlier session, we talked about keeping alert and being aware of what God was doing even when situations were difficult. Using Mark 13:33, we discussed how God wants our time, and this theme was revived. A. D. commented, "Following God's purpose for my life, not my purpose, is a struggle." We identified stages in life in relation to growing or maturing and noted that relationship with God also grows in stages. Someone asked, "What can you do differently to make better use of your time for the Lord?" C. O. stressed making time with the Lord a priority, and A. D. said we must give more attention to praising him.

In lesson seven, the discussion turned to stewardship of possessions. When the question was raised, "Does your giving grieve Jesus?" C. O. responded, "I don't tithe on time." He appeared to be extremely troubled and weighted by the thought. We discussed the idea of first fruits from the Old Testament and reassured him that setting his tithe aside before going out of town pleased God. The Israelites could not journey to Jerusalem every week. Session four concluded with an assignment for the following week. Participants were asked what they would do to show that they believed the lead verse in lesson eight: (Romans 12:3).

Session 5

Session five brought more discussion about being accountable for how we live and about the idea that we must grow. The lesson topics were "Accountable to God" and "The Purpose of Witnessing." A. D., C. H., S. R., C. M., C. O., and J. B. attended. The location was different; we met at the Whistle Stop, an ice cream parlor owned by one of the participants.

We met there for three reasons. First, it was Monday, July 5, and the church was closed for the holiday. We were able to acknowledge the holiday yet stay on schedule and avoid losing momentum toward growth. Second, the fellowship might produce conversation that would allow observation of group dynamics. We had reached a point in the maturing process where participants could comment on the program and/or self-assess. Taking the group to a different location would clarify the types of relationships that had formed. The facilitator encouraged C. O. to get directions from C. M., who needed transportation. One of the men was a newer member, and one was an older member; one had a car, and the other did not. They could communicate differently as they traveled to the location together. The third reason for having the session off site was to be a blessing to the owner—of course, we ate ice cream. After the facilitator put money in the tip glass, the others did the same.

The formal part of the session began with an overview of the process we had used thus far. Using index cards, participants wrote about their relationships with their disciple-makers and were given an opportunity to share the reflections.

C. H. shared an experience at a Laundromat. A lady's husband had recently died, and she questioned why God had taken him. C. H. told her that everything belonged to God and that the Lord had decided that he was ready to take her husband. Normally guarded, C. H. was surprised that she had so easily responded. Picking up the study book, she said, "From reading this I was able to respond to her. She said something to me that made me blush." C. H. was not aware of how much she had grown until a stranger complimented her. She could not remember the exact words because the feeling had overwhelmed her. The excitement on her face told more than a thousand words.

We covered "Accountable to God," then returned to the index cards and to the theme that people must be accountable to God for their relationships. Disciples must assume responsibility for growing rather than expecting others to reach out to them. To facilitate the discussion, we asked participants to share reflections on accountability from either of two perspectives or from both: the relationship with the disciple-maker and/or where the disciple-maker was with the disciple. Participants were asked not to use names, especially when referring to someone who was not present. In addition, they were admonished to focus on the relationship; the effectiveness of the triads would be revealed in what they had written on the index cards. The purpose was to have participants think through the process, which would lead to self-assessment. Toward the end of the session, they received a review sheet. (See appendix B.)

C. O. affirmed his discipleship though he had not started a relationship with a disciple-maker. He said he did not know how to do this. He added, "I don't know what to say." We talked about ways the disciple could approach the disciple-maker. C. M. affirmed himself as a disciple-maker. His relationship with a disciple was strong; in time of need, he would listen to the disciple and discuss the issue, extending comfort. Sharing continued with S. R. revealing herself as C. M.'s accountability partner. They had a mutual concern for family members, and she expressed the desire to pray more together.

A relationship began to develop for A. D. several months before our sessions, so she chose someone who was not a participant in the course.

She had connected to the disciple-maker with a hug during "one of my storms." Their relationship had grown from cordial greetings to frequent telephone conversations. When she needed to choose a disciple-maker, she realized the nature of that relationship. A. D. was comfortable talking with this person because of her warm and genuine spirit. She appreciated her teachings, her knowledge of the Word, and her friendship. J. B. was A. D.'s disciple-maker and was invited to the fellowship session. J. B. said that A. D. was now open to change so that God can use her. She believed that their relationship was where it should be; both were growing in the Lord.

After hearing others respond to the question about the progress of the disciple/disciple- maker relationships, C. H. said she felt safe to express her gut feelings within this relationship. Earlier she said that the relationship had not yet started. While listening to others in similar relationships, she was able to synthesize her position in a personal manner. The disciple-maker's knowledge and experience gave her confidence that there was someone she could call on at any time. She had begun to see a need to accept responsibility for initiating conversation that builds the rapport needed to grow a relationship. Later C. H. said that her best friend, who was unchurched, had attended church that weekend with her husband. Again, the environment allowed her to understand the process of transforming into a disciple and a disciple-maker.

S. R. hesitantly revealed that she did not know how to handle a longtime friend who was negative, gossiped about people, did not know the Lord, and hindered her growth. Fellow participants were eager to respond, but I asked her if she had prayed about it. When she said no, I told her to pray and to share with us at the next session. I asked the others not to respond at that point and suggested that disciple-makers guide disciples to communicate with God rather than take on his role. I said that disciple-makers should be available but should not assume the position of being the first resort since God is first.

Participants were assigned to be prepared to discuss any opportunities they had missed to witness between this session and the next. While we continued to pray and to become better stewards, our attention had turned from self to others. To promote self-assessment, participants were asked to:

- Compile a spiritual timeline.

- Consider their spiritual evolution since the sessions began.
- Refer to their life experiences rather than regurgitate the facilitator's information.

Session 6

"Qualifications for Witnessing" and "Jesus' Example of Witnessing" were the topics for the sixth session. C. H., C. M., S. R., D. C., and C. O. were present. We opened by discussing missed opportunities to witness. Before we listened to their accounts, participants were admonished to look for things within themselves that they could change. For example, they could consider the way they viewed their circumstances since situations may not change but the individual can. They were also asked to consider whether their attitudes were maturing. What was the evidence of that growth?

An exuberant C. H. told of witnessing to several people, while C. O. admitted to opportunities he did not take. S. R. said she had little chance to witness because she spent numerous hours babysitting infant twins. This discussion was less animated than those in previous sessions, and participants needed more prompting. The focus was on Christian maturity, which includes helping others because one has confidence in Jesus. C. O. confessed that he was not growing. He made a parallel to the Ethiopian eunuch in Acts 8:26–40. No one witnessed to the eunuch; he was reading the Word and Philip explained it to him. The eunuch accepted the truth and was baptized.

The remainder of the session dealt with scriptural interpretations, which affirmed participants' ability to draw from God's Word independent of the facilitator. The session concluded with an assignment to summarize the process toward Christian maturity. We discussed this, using the study book, which included the three segments of prayer, stewardship, and witnessing.

Session 7

The final session had the lowest attendance, with only A. D., C. H., and S. R. on hand. The topic was "Power to Witness," and we also summarized the process of growing toward Christian maturity. We asked three questions: Have you changed? What made you change? What has to happen to make you change? We also covered three questions in the study book.

Enthusiasm was low in this session. Several persons had told me that they would be absent, but I chose to stay on schedule for the sake of completing an academic process. The session would have been more effective with a majority of enrollees there to share. Several participants later said that they missed the time of sharing. To help participants gain closure, I hosted a time of fellowship in my home a month after the final session. S. R., C. O., and C. M. attended the Sunday afternoon event. The church was not involved, and we did not discuss course content. Still, participants felt no sense of closure.

Three months later an evaluation session was called for participants and for my colleagues to facilitate without bias that I might have. Focus group participants present included C. H., C. O., S. R., D. C., and A. D. The sixth participant, C. M., is a percussionist and went to choir rehearsal. A. M., V. S., and S. B. were the contextual associates on hand. V. S. sings in the choir and attended the first half of rehearsal before appearing for the second half of our session. S. B. was attending a gathering for the first time with other associates on this journey with her.

Summation Session

This session, held exactly three months after the course had ended, opened informally with members getting reacquainted and receiving updates on everyone's progress. C. O. observed that getting into heaven is hard to do. He thought that he was haphazardly reading the Bible and that this might be his problem. He admitted that he sometimes got depressed, and the group encouraged him to phone someone when he felt that way to revive his spirit. At this point, the session formally opened with a prayer.

Prior to more intimate sharing, participants completed the information sheet used for pre-assessment, this time for post-assessment purposes. (See the section in "Discipling Dilemma" after "Getting Started Corporately.") They also completed an evaluation sheet. (See appendix C.) To facilitate oral responses, participants were asked to consider where they were spiritually with where they recalled being three months before. This would allow the facilitator/researcher to capture the effects, if any, of their participation in the course. The pre-assessments were returned so participants could compare their spiritual postures before and after attending sessions.

After completing the pre-assessment during the first session, the researcher recorded on participants' information sheets verbatim responses regarding what prompted them to enroll. We did not refer to them again until this evaluation session. I described my role during the evaluation period as an observer, while a contextual associate, my colleague, facilitated the discussion. However, I provided input when appropriate.

Everyone was extremely attentive throughout the session as was true during the course. Conversation began with C. O. When he decided to join the group, he had been away from church for quite a few years. He was concerned about praying more effectively. He now prayed two or three times a day, including while driving or walking down the street. He reflected on the most recent revival held at our church, which focused on sin, acknowledging that he had come a long way in that area. C. O. professed a desire to be a follower; the more he learned, the wider the gate got. He was learning more about Satan and was being convicted. He realized that he needed to do a 180-degree turn, which would not take him around in a circle but would point him in a new direction. C. O. said that he attended many more classes and that he had made major progress. He affirmed his position as a disciple but was not yet a disciple-maker.

When A. M., as facilitator, asked what inspired him to get more serious, C. O. responded that he wanted to do right and abide by the Bible. He had to learn and move forward; he did not want to get discouraged. A. M. concluded that he was hungry for growing and for deepening. C. O. declared that he had come to hear about the Lord with a desire to disciple others but needed to learn more. He envisioned going to Africa to teach the people about God.

The next participant to offer reflections was S. R., who noted that she had both times declared herself a disciple and a disciple-maker. She enjoyed the challenge of trying, of following, and of doing what was right under God. A few people that she helped were not a part of the church; they had issues. She believed she needed still more growth to reach out to people she did not know. S. R. had spoken to people and was curious to see what their response would be. She said she could not attend all the sessions because of her work schedule. S. R. attended five of seven. She received a deeper understanding of what she already knew and thought that others should take the class.

Asked how long she had been maturing as a Christian, S. R. responded seven years. She grew up and was baptized as a child in this church. Her membership began on January 11, 1970. She added that she carried herself better although there were ups and downs in the maturing process. A. M. asked why she did not witness to strangers. S. R. replied that she was shy, more of a listener than a speaker. Once a conversation started, she would take part but did not easily initiate. A. M. probed into her written responses; S. R. professed to be a disciple-maker, but could she carry on a conversation about Christ? S. R. answered that she needed to work on that area. A. M. said her experience as a chaplain confirmed she might see a person only once. S. R. confessed that someone might ask her a question about the faith that she could not answer. A. M. suggested that she could try something like, "I don't know, but I do know that Jesus loves you." V. S. interjected the thought that inviting the person to attend Bible study with her might spark belief.

The researcher needed to do a little prompting to hear from the next person. D. C. began her response with a reflection on the first session from the notes on the pre-assessment sheet. She said that family members could be a problem and that they had criticized her for attending church so often. D. C. said she was glad she never stopped going to church. She had learned so much in eighteen years of being a member and attending the classes. Her husband was in the military and said the family would move back here when he retired. D. C. experienced depression because she did not want to return to her hometown. She could not come to classes because she was attending to the needs of family members. Looking down at the two information sheets, she solemnly declared, "Same thing—student and follower."

A perceptive A. M. counseled that she should realize that others were going through the same situation and that they needed to hear her testimony. D. C. replied that she now had told her family that she would not stop attending church. She had not previously exhibited such boldness. Others in the family were saved, but she felt that she was the one closest to Christ. A. M. then delved into D. C.'s ability to sever relationships if family interfered. Without hesitation, she affirmed that she could; she cited her desire to run to prayer and praise before Wednesday Bible study. She had not previously done that. She added that her motivation was more than prayer and praise; the testimonies were a help to her. A. M. inquired whether she had given her testimony. D. C. replied, "A few times but very briefly."

The next participant to share was C. H. She commenced by saying, "Praise the Lord," and thanked God for the opportunity. She declared that the course had done a lot for her because she had been starving, though trying to live by God's Word. She affirmed that her life had changed since taking the course. She said she needed a smaller group than Bible study offered; she had been attending Sunday school but not Bible study. Now she was involved in Sunday school, Bible study, and worship services.

Learning what God wanted her to be had been a constant challenge, and the answer was cloudy. When C. H. saw a "Maturing as a Christian" class advertised in the weekly newsletter, she decided that she needed to attend. She was now able to witness to strangers and had found they were experiencing the same thirst for growth and for knowledge of God. Now that she knew who he was, she lived to learn more. She recalled my telling her to wait; knowledge would come. She said it was coming but she was now fifty-eight and lonely. Learning about God was fulfilling, but if her closest relatives were not there, she felt empty. She had been at a point where she would not testify; she would pick and choose. Now she acknowledged God.

When A. M. pointed out that she had used the word *live* five or more times, C. H. retorted, "That's what you've gotta do; before I came here I was needy of the Word, trying to live the way God wants you to live." She recalled a session at which the facilitator suggested participants think of the marrow of their bone if they wondered whether they knew God deep within. She began to base her life on that idea. "I am just here and he is in my body," C. H. said. She mentioned attending weekly Bible study and Sunday school. She reflected on an employment change as well. She had owned her own business for four years and had to work on Sundays. She no longer had to do that because she worked as an assistant to a teacher of the handicapped. Referring to the revival C. O. attended, C. H. said she had realized when she was there that she was at the church a lot. She was taking piano lessons at the church, and a coworker let her use her keyboard. She professed her love for her church and said she was busy doing many other things now. She expressed gratitude for being able to come to Sunday school and to Bible study.

The thought that arrested A. M. was loneliness. She said that believers get lonelier the deeper they go into Christian maturity. Moving closer to God can push them further away from people. C. H. recollected that she had told a friend she wanted a closer relationship with God and that he had said this could mean loneliness. There may be nobody to share it with, but the Word is awesome. God showed her how to do things. She gave up the business and ended up with a job in the process. A minister in Charlotte, North Carolina, confirmed it. She said she came to church to get something, not just to be there; she came to see what God had for her. "You're committed," A. M. concluded.

The reflections continued with an exuberant hallelujah from A. D. She expressed her emotion verbally and with teary eyes. She sobbed off and on the entire time she spoke. She praised God for good times and for bad times, something she had done before attending the sessions. But the course confirmed the practice. She had also learned to sit still long enough to hear God's answers to her prayers. She acknowledged asking God for his will rather than for things that she wanted. A. D. said she had not arrived and had a long way to go.

She could visualize the importance of growing up in the church because she didn't have family roots in one. Her mother was a spiritual woman, though she did not often go to church. A. D. felt she had missed a great deal but could give experiences to her grandson, whom she was raising. She said that when she did not want to go, her grandson would say, "Tomorrow is Sunday. Got to go to church" or "Uncle has been missing church quite a while." She felt strongly about keeping this seven-year-old in church. She recognized that he was paying attention. One communion Sunday he said, "This is the day I get more blood in me; I'm glad he's my daddy." A. D. confirmed being where she needed to be despite missing growing up in church. She was determined that her grandson would not miss the experience. She proudly noted that he had asked to pray earlier that day.

Concerning maturity, A. D. had learned to ask herself where to go in the Bible to make sense out of what was going on in her life. She now looked for God's purpose in her circumstances. She found comfort in knowing that he was Lord. While she did not think she could share her faith with everybody, she said she would be able to discuss it. She recalled a person who told her that she wanted to leave her husband. A. D. was ambivalent but responded with what she had learned. "God helps you so much that you have to give," she said. A. D. sobbed as she said that she loved the Lord.

She was not satisfied with her attendance at Bible study but remained committed to going to Sunday school every week. She took her grandson, who liked it. In addition, when she heard somebody recite a Scripture verse she could finish it. She professed to having acquired much from our sessions. The end of the course "messed me up," she said. "It was a helpful guide." She said that when she looked back at difficult situations, God reminded her that he could handle them. A. D. expressed remorse for letting God down. She did not want to leave Virginia to go to her hometown in another state because she did not want to leave the church. Her appreciation for biblical teaching was profound.

When A. M. asked if she considered herself a disciple-maker, A. D. responded with a firm no. A. M. told her that she could be and cited her grandson and the lady who wanted to leave her husband. A. D. had not considered that. Upon reflection, she recalled a visit by a friend from her hometown. While worshiping together at church, A. D. "caught the Holy Spirit," startling her longtime friend. The friend never said anything to A. D., but the friend's husband told A. D. how she had reacted. The friend now sought Scripture advice from A. D. during long- distance calls. A. M. admonished A. D. not to lose her sensitivity.

The researcher asked that the discussion include participants' involvement in church ministries since taking the course. A. D. was not satisfied because she did not want to take half steps. She wanted to become involved in the women's ministry but did not have the time. Her reasons included work, her grandson, and a need to balance activities. She loved to sing and was a part of the music ministry. When I asked what she wanted to do in the women's ministry, she said she wanted to work with women who had drug problems and were coming out of prison. She did not feel she could commit to that now.

C. O. acknowledged a need to do something for others and pointed to kids and missions. V. S. suggested prayer; she said that God had led him to it. She also asked about his spiritual gifts, noting that deficiencies can harm an individual and a ministry. C. O. said he wanted to do more than take pictures for the public relations committee.

Being a part of an intimate discussion group helped participants to self-reflect while listening to others. For example, after C. O. had spoken, A. D. revealed that God had prophesied to her what ministry she would do. The university teaching position she held ended when a program was severed; this led to employment working with ex-offenders who had addiction problems. God allowed her to become an adjunct professor and placed her where he wanted.

C. H. admitted that she was not involved in any ministry, then mentioned two opportunities to unite with others at the church to study the Bible on Wednesday night and Sunday morning. She said she had not had a desire to take part in anything. I asked God to guide her to where she was supposed to go. She attributed to God her working with handicapped children as a student assistant. This was a new position in her school, and she had told the teacher she assisted that some tasks she had assigned were inappropriate and interfered with her doing what the principal hired her to do. I suggested that she see increased participation in Bible study and Sunday school as involvement in the nurture and disciple-making ministry. She concurred after pondering the idea.

S. R. continued her involvement with ushering, Sunday school, and Bible study; she was concerned about not overburdening herself. D. C. remained attached to the usher board. Others commented on her smile, implying that her greeting at the church doors was important.

Feeling an increased desire to do something in the community or the church, A. M. surmised a commissioning of sorts. V. S. deduced that everyone had a yearning to grow and to know more. Though she did not participate in the sessions as a contextual associate, reading the study resource made her want to learn more. She cautioned participants not to allow anything to obstruct them. She said that as they were maturing, they should remember the steps in the process. The foundation had been laid; now they had to assume responsibility for building the house. V. S. told them to keep their burning desire and to give testimony. She finished by adding that Satan takes our joy because of a lack of boldness and that God forgives.

I refocused attention on the contextual associates, asking them to consider the initial focus of the developmental design, then compare thoughts from the inception to the evaluation session. A. M. said the project was designed to help people move from being disciples to disciple-makers. The course was part of the process. She was not certain how many people had reached the next level; she also speculated that some had but did not think so. The responsibility to be disciple-makers had been made clear; participants had a desire to be disciple-makers and were focused on this goal, and a developmental process allowed people not only to make disciples but to go beyond the walls of the church. Judging from the evaluation session, A. M. concluded that some still need that little extra push.

Recognizing the absence of functioning triads throughout the discussion, before closing I asked how many were communicating within a group that included disciple, disciple-maker, and coach. With no immediate responses, I tried another approach, asking whether anyone had initiated a call to a disciple-maker. A. D. had left prior to my question; all the others shook their heads no. I affirmed their participation in the process and asked A. M. for a closing prayer.

V. S. had also left a few minutes before closing and had not responded to my query. The following day via telephone, she shared her perspective. Though she did not hear A. M. or later speak with her, their responses were quite comparable. The difference was that A. M. had functioned as an outside observer while V. S. had preconceived notions as an active member of the congregation. V. S. admitted that she thought people would come, go through the sessions, and say they understood the content. She did not realize that they wanted to go to another spiritual level. People wanted the smaller setting; they wanted something more personal. The sessions were clearly personal and that made them work.

The facilitator put a lot in and received a lot more than expected. She saw proof in participants' expressions and in the fact that people she had not believed would speak in group settings were sharing. She surmised that they began the sessions thinking they were unworthy but thought they had something to offer at the end.

I encouraged V. S. to continue to reflect until she finished. She said becoming disciple-maker was the top priority of participants. They had stopped to consider what they should be doing and did not jump into anything. They knew to proceed in steps and not to take on overly burdensome duties. They had been given a measure of self-assurance and learned that they were important. They now came not only on Sunday morning but throughout the week. I do not think they would have taken that step had it not been for the sessions they attended. V. S. assured me that they would ask for more. I said that had happened before the final session.

V. S. also noted the importance of keeping participants interested and asked, "How do we go further and beyond?" She acknowledged their need for a little more self-assurance. I recalled C. O.'s discouragement and visualization of the narrow gate. V. S. confirmed that he would not have been able to share that in a larger setting.

The next step in the process of Christian maturity at this church was to merge participants into church ministries. Since we have so many opportunities for involvement, we encouraged assimilation rather than promote new ministries. Participants were urged to explore what the congregation offered. Continuing the course would have contradicted the purpose of getting people out of the pews and into ministry. I was also concerned about participants becoming dependent on me rather than on God.

V. S. suggested that the closing portion of the course could be titled "Understanding Spiritual Gifts." She reminded me of an inventory I did in Bible study showing where each gift was illustrated in Scripture. Using this approach, participants would get a better perception of where they might fit into the congregation. However, none of the course participants attended those sessions as part of Wednesday Bible study or the advanced Bible institute when they were offered.

V. S. revisited participants' desire to mature; the course was not fulfilling since they needed more. We have more. I insisted that we should not develop something new, and she agreed that studying the Word worked and that this is what participants need. A missing component in our church is the chance for people to talk in small groups as a part of a routine study process. We do a lot of teaching, but the ongoing opportunity for intimate engagement needs more emphasis.

Notes

1. George Barna, *Growing True Disciples: New Strategies for Producing Genuine Followers of Christ* (Colorado Springs, Colorado: WaterBrook Press, 2001), 19.
2. Ron Bennett and John Purvis, *The Adventure of Discipling Others: Training in the Art of Disciplemaking* (Colorado Springs, Colorado: Navpress, 2003), 10.
3. John Koessler, *True Discipleship: The Art of Following Jesus* (Chicago: Moody Press, 2003), 19–20.
4. Luke Timothy Johnson, *The Writings of the New Testament: An Interpretation* (Minneapolis: Fortress Press, 1999), 521.
5. Leland Ryken, James C. Wilhoit, and Tremper Longman III, ed., *Dictionary of Biblical Imagery* (Downers Grove, Illinois: InterVarsity Press, 1998), 310–311.
6. John Koessler, *True Discipleship: The Art of Following Jesus* (Chicago: Moody Press, 2003), 19–20.
7. R. V. G. Tasker, *John Tyndale New Testament Commentaries* (Grand Rapids, Michigan: Eerdmans Publishing Company, 1995), 174–175.
8. William M. Ramsay, *The Westminster Guide to the Books of the Bible* (Westminster John Knox Press: Louisville, Kentucky, 1994), 292.
9. Adapted from Ron Bennett and John Purvis, *The Adventure of Discipling Others: Training in the Art of Disciplemaking* (Colorado Springs, Colorado: Navpress, 2003), 9.
10. Nice, Karim, and Charles W. Bryant. "How Catalytic Converters Work" November 8, 2000. HowStuffWorks.com. <http://www.howstuffworks.com/catalytic-converter.htm> accessed, February 5, 2014.
11. Barbara A. F. Brehon, *Nurture for Baptist Churches: Maturing as a Christian* (Nashville, Tennessee: Sunday School Publishing Board, 2004), 1–40.
12. John D. Ogletree Jr., *Moving to the Next Level: Becoming a Fully-Developing Follower of Christ* (Lithonia, Georgia: Orman Press, 2001), 1-155.
13. Brehon, 1.

Bibliography

Barna, George. *Growing True Disciples: New Strategies for Producing Genuine Followers of Christ.* Colorado Springs, Colorado: WaterBrook Press, 2001.

Bennett, Ron and John Purvis. *The Adventure of Discipling Others: Training in the Art of Disciplemaking.* Colorado Springs, Colorado: Navpress, 2003.

Brehon, Barbara A. F. *Nurture for Baptist Churches: Maturing as a Christian.* Nashville: Sunday School Publishing Board, 2004.

Johnson, Luke Timothy. *The Writings of the New Testament: An Interpretation.* Minneapolis: Fortress Press, 1999.

Koessler, John. *True Discipleship: The Art of Following Jesus.* Chicago: Moody Press, 2003.

Nice, Karim, and Charles W. Bryant. "How Catalytic Converters Work" November 8, 2000. HowStuffWorks.com. http://www.howstuffworks.com/catalytic-converter.htm, accessed February 5, 2014.

Ramsay, William M. *The Westminster Guide to the Books of the Bible.* Louisville, Kentucky: Westminster John Knox Press, 1994.

Ryken, Leland; James C. Wilhoit, and Tremper Longman III, ed. *Dictionary of Biblical Imagery.* Downers Grove, Illinois: InterVarsity Press, 1998.

Tasker, R. V. G. *John Tyndale New Testament Commentaries.* Grand Rapids, Michigan: Eerdmans Publishing Company, 1995.

More from the Author

*Write the vision and make it plain. (*Habakkuk 2:23).

I thank the Lord for the signal to begin again. He has helped me to have published the following:

1. *Reach Me with SMILES: A Handbook for Developing Disciple Makers*, Orman Press, 2005, revised 2014.
2. Sunday School Publishing Board of the National Baptist Convention: one book (a); twelve articles (b); and six curricula (c, d).
    a. The introduction to *Singles: Strengthened, Secured, and Spirit-Filled*, 2007
    b. *Christian Education Informer*
        i. "Becoming a Teaching Church: A 21st Century Need," September–November 1998
        ii. "Tutorial Ministry," March–May 2000
        iii. "Summer Enhancement Ministry," June–August 2000
        iv. "Tutorial Ministry: More Than a Program," September–November 2000
        v. "Rediscovering the Joy of Teaching," March–May 2001
        vi. "Increasing Teacher Effectiveness: Reach One," December 2001–February 2002*
        vii. "Christian Classroom Discipline," December 2001–February 2002
        viii. "Why Teach Doctrine?," September–November 2003
        ix. "Mission-Minded Ministry," December 2003–February 2004
        x. "Accountability: A Godly Mandate," Spring 2010

        xi. "No Substitute for Christian Teaching," September–November 2012
        xii. "Celebrating Biblical Women: Daughters of Destiny," March–May 2013
   c. Nurture for Baptists (2004)
        i. "Maturing as a Christian," Summer 2004
        ii. "Questions About the Faith," September–November 2004
        iii. "Growing in the Faith," Spring 2005
        iv. "Guidelines for Godly Living," Fall 2005
   d. Vacation Bible School (2005–06)
        i. "Operation Victory, Ephesians 6:10–17, Intermediate Lessons," 2005
        ii. "Power On! With Jesus, Acts 1:8 and 2:1–4," 2006

My spiritual growth makes me a work in progress; I am ever evolving, forever growing.

About the Author

Barbara A. F. Brehon is associate pastor of Beulah Baptist Church in Tappahannock, Virginia, reading specialist for the Essex County Public Schools, and missionary partner with Kenya. She authored Reach Me with SMILES: A Handbook for Developing Disciple Makers and numerous articles. She preaches and teaches God's Word with fervor and sincerity.

CPSIA information can be obtained at www.ICGtesting.com
Printed in the USA
BVOW01s2056280514

354343BV00003B/24/P